Breaking the Cycle

HOPE ❋ RESILIENCE ❋ GRATITUDE

Two Little Girls and Their Rise to Success

Christine Beckwith
Dr. Wendy L. Wright, FNP

Susan —

We broke the cycle didn't we —

20/20 Vision Press

Wendy Wright DNP

Breaking the Cycle / Christine Beckwith and Dr. Wendy L. Wright
First edition, 20/20 Vision Press, an imprint of Manifest Publishing

ISBN 978-1-944913-48-9

Contents

Dedicated to our Parents

Four People Who Truly Broke the Cycle

Wendy's Dedication:

For Howard and Carolee

For many reasons, this is the easiest yet the most difficult part of the book to write. During the final phases of writing this book, my mom Carolee (Hoyt) Hurd passed away at the age of seventy years. She had lived with me, my husband Eric, and son Dillon for the past seventeen years. While I had known that her death would occur sooner rather than later, nothing quite prepares you for the loss of your mom and what it feels like to lose both parents. My mom was called home on December 31, 2018 to join my dad, Howard L. Hurd who had died sixteen years prior at the age of 62.

This book is dedicated to my parents *Howard* and *Carolee*; the two people who truly **broke the cycle**. My mom was eighteen when she gave birth to me, and my dad twenty-eight—so young to be parents. Mom was still a kid herself, learning as she went along.

While neither parent graduated from high school nor went to college, you would never have known. They pushed us toward education, even when they had never experienced it themselves. They loved unconditionally, even when I gave them so many reasons not to. They sacrificed all they had to enable my sister Becky and me to succeed.

They taught us many life lessons: what it means to work hard for the things you want; what it means to be honest and kind; how to give more than you receive; and how to put others first. I am truly grateful for their love, kindness, and sacrifices. I am also blessed to have been able to tell them both before their death how much I appreciated all they did for me.

I love and miss you both more than I can ever put into words. I hope you are dancing, laughing, and loving Heaven with all who went before you.

This book is also dedicated to a few other special people in my life.

To my son Dillon: whom I stayed on bedrest for eighteen weeks to have. He is my biggest accomplishment.

To my husband Eric: a man who has stood by me even when he should not have. He takes the backseat to allow me to shine. He has sacrificed to make sure Dillon and I have what we need. Thirty-one years of marriage to me has certainly not been an easy ride. Thanks for sticking around.

To my sister Becky: our relationship has come a long way. From our endless fights in childhood to our spats in adulthood, I could not think of anyone better to share this crazy thing we call life. Just a bit of advice Becky, you should have been an FBI agent😊.

To my teachers, my staff, my patients, my friends, and my colleagues—thank you for always cheering me on and rooting for this little girl from a trailer park in New Hampshire. You gave me hope and a future. For that, I am eternally grateful.

Last, to Christine, my childhood friend: writing this book has been a great process with you by my side. Your global thinking and perpetual optimism have pushed me into writing things I didn't think I could. Together, along with our parents before us, we have *Broken the Cycle* and I could not think of anyone better to share this journey with.

Christine's Dedication:

For Merle and Sandra

It is simple to mirror Wendy's sentiments about her beloved parents, whom I also loved and admired. In writing about a theme like **Breaking the Cycle**, we knew we wanted to share our collective, close and parallel stories that drew on our inner belief systems, our wiring, if you will, of hope and resilience and all things that allowed us to survive and thrive.

It will not come as a surprise that I believe my portion of this book should be dedicated to the two people who truly **Broke the Cycle**: my mother, *Sandra Heath Stiles* and my father, *Merle Robert Stiles* Each has incredible stories of their own; stories of triumph over adversity that are, in many ways, far harder and steeper than my own. Their successes happen because of their ability to come together as a team, in partnership, and to work towards a common goal. They inched their way out of poverty to give their daughters (me being their middle daughter) a better life than either endured.

To know my mother and father is to know that they do not see themselves as victims. There are few times I have seen true, lasting sadness expressed by either of them. They are the salt of the earth, true blue, hard-working people who simply made a conscious decision to give their best and keep their lives moving in a direction that allowed them to provide, regardless of their own sacrifices along the way.

For that sacrifice, I cannot possibly express in words the deep, sincere gratitude and admiration I feel for them. They are my heroes and they always will be. I love them both incredibly.

Thank you for setting an example to follow, for the times I didn't appreciate your sacrifices, and for giving me an environment where my internal wiring could thrive, where belief could be born out of little, and prosper into the big dreams I am still chasing. I love you both! I will honor you for the rest of our lives and ensure that the world knows how two incredible people redefined the world in such a way that it created in me a hope that has lasted a lifetime.

To my son, Jagger James Beckwith and my boyfriend of over a decade, Cory Michael Parker: I easily and sincerely appreciate how both of you support and fuel my life in such a way that the values and beliefs, set into motion during my childhood, have been able to live and thrive with you as my primary source of both. I love you both immensely.

To my two sisters from whom I draw much of my sense of family and comfort: I am grateful knowing that I will always be able to look to my right or to my left and feel their true support. They are both incredible examples of championing perseverance in life, overcoming, and surviving. I love them both!

I am also incredibly grateful to my closest friends (too many to mention by name) but you know who you are. My inner circle of support has seen me at my lowest and my best and never judged me on either side of that fence.

To the incredible staff of my company 20/20 Vision for Success: I cannot thank them enough for being on a journey to my dreams and having them take pride and ownership in our pursuit for success. *You are all champions to an incredible cause of helping change the lives of so many.*

It is from all these sources of incredibly intimate love in my life that I can give outwardly so much of myself to others. Without these people I would not be who I am today or where I am today. I am fortunate to have so many incredible people on this journey.

"So very thankful, incredibly grateful, and unbelievably blessed."

–UNKNOWN SOURCE

Christine's Why

As I look back today on the long journey begun in childhood on Parade Road, I clearly see the meandering path from then to now, filled with twists and turns that intertwine with the experiences of my childhood friend, Wendy Wright. Our lives have taken parallel roads, even from the start. This came into focus for me in recent years when, after a chance meeting in our hometown, we reconnected and traced some astonishing similarities.

We have shared geographical proximity; neither of us has moved far from our roots. We also have taken eerily similar emotional journeys and are wired much the same. Certainly, our parallel lives, born out of different incidents and experiences, have taken completely different tracks, yet each of us have come to achieve incredible professional success.

I can see now, looking back, that we made difficult choices in our lives, that we had extreme responsibility placed upon us (possibly self-generated but nonetheless real), that we became leaders amidst our peers, and we took on dependents amongst our families.

I can see now, looking back, how we made crucial professional decisions that would propel us into the public eye. After long walks for each of us down our respective professional paths, who could predict that fate would bring us back to our hometown at the same time? Who could predict the irony of our meeting at the very school where we struggled to find financing for our secondary education? Who could predict that we shared the same purpose: To give away scholarship monies to students following in our footsteps?

That day we stood together, each grown with huge lives, and yet called to give back and pay forward to others in need. That day, we were two poor little girls no longer poor, no longer afraid, and no longer without a voice.

Today, we live our lives wrought with responsibility, a weight that might cripple the average person, and yet we stand strong, we are calloused, we are confident.

We are always moving, always working, always serving our businesses and students, rarely resting, feeling as if, were we to stop, the empires we have built would tumble down, or we ourselves would unravel.

We are perhaps weathered and resolved, experienced and aged. We are women who look back to where it all began and see that we have a story to tell.

The steps we've taken have been careful, intentional, and always mindful of survival and success. Concise steps taken by two little girls who grew up a few hundred yards apart, both poor and hopeful of a life to be lived, a world to be traveled, and dreams to be chased. Sometimes we stepped out on extreme blind faith and bravado; often we were fueled by fear.

And now, in finding one another again, we know it is our calling and our yearning, equally so, to give back to all girls and women who need hope, direction, lessons and leadership.

Today, we are bringing you our shared stories. We pause to reflect, to journal, and to share our life stories so others may follow our compass with greater confidence in their ability to create a better life. We come to you with the knowledge we hold close, as it is the best of our life lessons:

We are proven.

We are celebrated.

We have achieved amazing results.

We welcome you to join us.

Break the Cycle of your life just as we rose from the trailer parks of our childhood to triumph as adult women.

Wendy's Why

As a little girl growing up in Smoky Hollow Trailer Park, my greatest joy was reading. I was an avid reader from the day my mom introduced me to books at the age of two. When mom and dad would take us shopping, my sister would ask for a toy, and I always asked for a book.

I meticulously cared for every book I owned; always using a bookmark to avoid bending the pages. I had my books organized in alphabetical order by author and even maintained a catalog of each book I owned so that I could locate them easily in my tiny bedroom. I read every book from the *Nancy Drew* and *Hardy Boys* series. I devoured books written about *Laura Ingalls Wilder* and her childhood. I loved anything written by *Judy Blume*. Reading for me was a pleasure. It took me to places I dreamed I would someday be able to visit.

As a child, I wanted to write a book; to put my thoughts into words and see them printed on a page. I never imagined that it would be possible, or that I would be asked to write a book about my life. I published my first book when I was 30 years old. I wrote it during the eighteen weeks that I was on bedrest while pregnant with my son Dillon.

I had developed a set of *cue cards* to help nurse practitioner students learn how to conduct and document a physical examination on an adult patient. I had self-published and used them with my students in a physical assessment course that I was teaching at Simmons University. The students repeatedly asked me if they could buy them, and the idea for a book was launched.

I knew they were helpful to nurse practitioner students, but when does a busy woman, working both a full time and a part-time job, have time to write a book? Forced bedrest gave me that time.

After writing the Adult History and Physical Examination book, a colleague of mine requested the opportunity to reproduce and sell them through her company. Today, this physical assessment book is in its ninth edition and continues to serve as a valuable resource for nurse practitioner students throughout the country.

Back to why I am here with you today. Christine Stiles Beckwith and I grew up in adjacent trailer parks, on Parade Road, in the small little town of Meredith, New Hampshire. As children, we worked together at an arcade. Christine was the same age as my sister and had a peer group different from mine. After graduating high school, we went our separate ways. We didn't see each other for the next twenty years.

The next time our paths crossed was a beautiful night in June 2007. We were both back at our former high school to award a monetary scholarship to a graduating senior from our alma mater. Christine had founded her scholarship in honor of her childhood friend, who had recently died of AIDS, and I founded mine in honor of my father, who had recently died from gallbladder cancer. I remember seeing her that night and thinking to myself, *This woman has her act together. Her scholarship award speech was moving and captivating. She was composed and the epitome of a professional.*

For the next few years, we would come together every June to award these scholarships. Two to three years later, we connected on Facebook, and as they say in the business, the rest is history. I am a believer that things happen as they should. It was meant to be.

It remains amazing to me how similar our lives were, and we didn't even know it.

We lived only a few miles from one another. Despite the proximity, our paths had never crossed until that day in June.

On the day we finally got together to discuss this book, we pulled up to a local restaurant and parked next to each other. Neither of us could believe our eyes. We were driving the same SUV and in the same color.

We were moms to only children, our beloved sons.

We had given birth in the same hospital.

We were patients of the same nurse practitioner.

We had both created a career in public speaking.

The similarities were comforting but eerie.

For the past 50 years, I have told very few people about my life. Those close enough for me to let in on my past have often said to me, "You need to write a book. People will read it. You are an inspiration."

I never believed it.

As Christine and I reminisced about our past, we laughed, and we cried.

We spoke about our childhood, and we each understood the importance of this conversation.

We instinctively understood each other's struggles and how hard we had to work to get to this point in our lives.

We understood that the work was not just physical work but emotional work, as well.

We vowed that day to write this book.

If truth be told, as a young adult, I was too embarrassed to speak about my past and to tell my story. I had worked so hard to escape my past and **break the cycle** of poverty, that I did everything I could to avoid speaking of it.

While this may sound terrible to many of you (don't get me wrong, it sounds terrible to me as I write it), there was a lot of pain associated with these memories, and it was easier to bury and ignore the embarrassment than address it.

As I have gotten older and spent time in self-reflection, I have come to realize that I have absolutely NOTHING of which to be ashamed. I had two parents who loved me; two parents who did everything they could to provide for us. No, they didn't have fancy clothes, cars, or a big house—but honestly, they had more than most. They were proud people; salt-of-the-earth, give you the shirts off their backs kind of people. They were simple folk who were filled with love for their children. They did the best they could to see us succeed. I was truly blessed to have all that I did. It is so much more than many.

Today, my past is a badge of honor. I wear it proudly. Without it, I would not be the person I am. My past has taught me to be kind yet assertive, to treat people with respect and not be stepped on, to give back to those less fortunate, and to leave this world a better place than it was when I came into it.

Some of my greatest joys have come from being able to take care of my family; to take my mom and dad on vacations; to experience Hawaii through the eyes of my mother—a place she had always wanted to visit but was never able to afford. To give my mom and dad a home during the last days of his life; to have my mom live with me for the seventeen years after Dad's death and to give my mother the gift of taking her last breath in my home, as she had asked to do during the final week of her life.

I still have work to do, but I have **broken the cycle**.

Christine and I have **broken the cycle**.

We are blessed to have clothes on our backs, food on our tables, and the ability to provide for our families. We are so lucky to not worry about how we are going to eat or feed our children; something our parents had to worry about frequently.

We pray that as we take you along our journey, you find hope and happiness. We pray that you come to find inspiration for your life from our humble beginnings and by what we have been able to accomplish. Come along on our journey!

CHAPTER 1

The Neighborhood

Hope

"a feeling of expectation and desire for a certain thing to happen"

Christine

As I sit on a plane for the umpteenth flight of my career, a little girl is seated next to me for her first flight. She's excited, phone in hand, ready to record the first of her lifetime of memories, and I am enraptured by her enthusiasm. I remember experiencing that glorious, new discovery feeling when I was her age.

Sophia is her name. We talk, and I share what I do. She asks me to show her what my books look like, so I gift her the two I am carrying with me on this trip. I tell her to pay forward the lessons in each. We take a photo, and I know she will be a great soldier of my words. I can just tell.

Meeting Sophia was delightful, and as I settled into the rest of the flight, my thoughts quite naturally turned to my childhood...

Hope. Dream chasing. Work ethic.

I claim these character traits, each forged during my elementary school years. Many contests would be entered: dance competition, student council campaigns, science fairs, gymnastic and other athletic tournaments. Every time I thought about entering a race, I became excited. I would visualize the event that would culminate whatever period of practice and preparation I had, and I could see that time would allow me to hone whatever skill I needed. And somehow, vision became reality as I would find myself winning.

Looking back now, I realize I have always dreamed big. I've been called dramatic by many people and often not as a compliment. I must own it because it is a truth. I view this as an art and a strength. An innate predisposition for drama, used for doing good, to tell a story, to make people laugh, to create excitement, is a great personality trait to have. It can also be a powerful, emotion evoking weapon if misused. It has always been easy to get a group of people behind me.

The point I want to come back to is that I was born with hope and excitement for life in me and, to this day, wake up excited and eager to live life. I believe this enthusiasm is a gift, and because hope for greater things and bigger things is ever present, I can lead others to the same belief. What others call drama; I know to be passion that shines through all things I do.

Despite having a long list of disadvantages and hurdles to overcome, I've always felt certain I had this big life in front of me. In everything I do, I am aware of my deficits. And yet, somehow, the way forward is found. I remember as a child nursing hurts no youngster should endure and thinking, *I will not be denied. I don't care what others say, how others tell me it can't be done. I don't believe them. I know they are wrong.*

We lived the furthest from my school one could possibly live and still attend. The town line was a stone's throw away. We were on the last street in town, so the school bus picked us up first. It made for a long ride as the bus wove through the back roads of our rural community, skirting the peripheral of a mill town that had evolved past its glory days. Over half the property in town was owned by wealthy out-of-staters who came for the camps cresting the edges of our 20 miles of lakes. We sat in a valley of the greatest terrain in the northeast, a latch key to the enormous White Mountains.

Our town was a picture of opposites, filled with wealth—those who came from their lofty lives in Massachusetts to vacation—and the impoverished Townies. Opulence to penury teetered in both directions, with few people in between. Affluence created segregation, even among the townies, where wealthy business owners of hotels, restaurants, and big businesses thrived amid the rest of us who lived in the trailer parks and camps on the exterior looking in.

I do not remember a time when I was not aware of lack. I was keenly aware of kids like me who could not afford much. I longed for people to see the real me, to look past the rough exterior, to look beyond the shoes from K-mart. I thought early on, if they saw ME and my heart, that they would look past the hurt I felt inside for the things I was limited to in life by money. I didn't know for a very long time how inconsequential these things and how misguided it was to allow 'fitting in' to weigh so heavy on my heart.

Our classrooms were arranged around 'aptitude' groups. I had an inside out view of the harsh cruelty of other children because I was placed in a group made up mostly of the affluent kids. All day, our group moved from one class to the next together. The rich kids in my group would laugh and mock other kids who didn't have the designer clothes. They mistreated kids who were different; children with societal inversions like shyness, and those who had hygiene issues (no doubt from their home environments as I knew at least six of my fellow students who had no running water or electricity in their homes).

I remember one day while waiting for the school bus, I saw a younger girl have her winter hat torn off her head by one of this so-called more affluent class. They passed around the hat, like a cruel game of keep away, while the little girl wailed for them to return it to her.

She was the daughter of one of my mom and dad's coworkers, and I had just hung out with them Saturday night at my home while our parents played cards. There was nothing physically harmful, but it was embarrassing, emotionally taunting, and hurtful.

At first, I didn't think I could do anything to help. After all, there were three boys my age laughing and continuing the taunting, throwing the hat back and forth between them. Then, before my mind could catch up with my feet, I seized the hat mid-toss from the clutches of one of the boys. With a great shove and a forceful glare, I pushed him to the ground. The other kids laughed. I turned and returned the hat to my friend. She looked at me with tears streaming down her face and managed a slight smile as she reclaimed her hat, placing it firmly on her head.

I walked away angry and shaking. I quickened my pace and ran around the corner of the building where I stood with my back to the wall of the school. It was cold outside, and I could hear the bus coming, and I was crying. For a

4

truly important moment, my body had taken me for a ride. I was on auto pilot. As I felt the adrenaline leaving my body, a teacher came around the corner to tell me I am a good girl and that I need to get in line for the bus.

Having the bird's-eye view from the 'high aptitude' group for the ten years of my school career, placed me between fitting in and not. I became the unexpected diplomat moving in both circles, the unaccepted and the privileged. Over the years, I kind of saw myself as the school yard superhero. I was always watching.

Many of the parents of the ostracized children were my neighbors and my parents' co-workers at the mill. These were my Saturday night playmates while our families socialized. I was friends with everyone as if, by example, I could show others how kids were kids, and nobody deserved to be bullied.

I believe my friends among the privileged kids did not like that I reminded them of their own lack of importance. True fact: their parents were rich, but they had no more than any other kid their age. Having stuff given to you does not make you better than anybody else. My attitude was to shame them if they were stuck up, and I didn't care if they liked it or not. What they chose to do with their advantage in life would determine who they became. I believe I knew, even then, that these early struggles would not define my life but rather enrich it. And somehow, I knew another truth, even though as a child I could not have expressed any of this: that abusing the significant advantages they had as children could, and likely would, become challenges to overcome in later life.

Remaining hopeful and living a life filled with hope has proven to be both my greatest strength and one of my greatest challenges. Maintaining blind faith in life's goodness is not easy. I have not always made the best choices or taken the right actions. And when missteps happened, it was hope, an internal faith that kept me hanging on. Having hope let me dream of a different future I couldn't yet see.

What we hope for wills us to better destinations. I am a believer in our internal compass. We go to where we look. When we look or hope for better, we find it.

When we believe nothing better will come, we are willing for the bad and attracting it. When we speak aloud words of dismay and words of hate or negativity, we draw in those who think similarly. Take care because there begins a spiral difficult to reverse. Avoid, whenever possible, an environment wrought with negative people, thoughts, and outcomes.

We have the power to define our destiny. You must put that theory into action to believe it.

Wendy

I AM AMAZED BY HOW MANY of Christine's childhood memories are similar to mine despite occurring years and miles apart. Who could have known that something which seemed so simple or insignificant at the time could create a permanent scar in our psyche forty-years later?

I know I speak for Christine and myself when I say that many of these childhood memories left an indelible mark on our lives but also helped to shape us into who and what we have become today. They have made us tough yet compassionate, resilient yet sensitive, grateful and maybe most importantly, hopeful. We have hope. It is that hope that gets us up and out of bed every day and guides us in all that we do; hope, not only for our own lives and the lives of our children, but for those of our employees, coworkers, friends, and patients.

One morning when I was 9 years old, I left our trailer to head to the bus stop for school. Upon arriving at the bus stop, a boy, about 5 years older than me, began teasing me. He grabbed my purse and refused to give it back. It wasn't the first time that he had done such a thing to me and others. I was sad, humiliated, and unsure of what to do. I asked him repeatedly to give it back but despite my pleas, he refused.

I fought desperately to avoid crying because I knew, from previous experience with him, that if I cried, it would only make things worse. I knew that crying would only give him pleasure from my pain. So many other kids were standing there watching, yet no one offered to help. They were also afraid of him and his bullying.

Out of the corner of my eye, I see a woman approaching. It was my mother. She had seen it all; the bullying, taunting, and teasing, that look of sadness and humiliation on my face.

Every morning, after mom walked us out the door, she returned to her bedroom to watch me and my sister walk to the bus stop. She would sit in her chair and watch until we got onto the bus when she would wave and send us a kiss goodbye.

As my mom approached us that morning, she was dressed in her flannel nightgown with curlers in her hair and a bandana on her head. I watched half in awe and half embarrassed as she literally grabbed this boy by the neck and demanded he give me back my purse. He did so immediately; he was scared. She also told him that she would be watching him every day, and if he ever so much as laid a hand on me again, she would kill him. And while I knew she really didn't mean it, she meant it. She was that momma bear protecting her cub.

I bet many of you have felt these same feelings with your loved ones. I know I have felt them with my own son. I often say, the only reason I would ever wear orange with horizontal stripes is if someone hurt my son.

How different, yet how similar my experiences were to Christine's.

Christine speaks about the impact that bullying has had on her and how these events have left marks on her life. For both of us, they have also instilled hope; hope for a world that is kinder and gentler than that which we have witnessed, hope that somehow, what happened to us wouldn't happen to someone else.

While I would like to tell you that being hopeful comes easily to me, it doesn't. My brain is somehow programmed to expect the worst and pray for the best. I do wonder if this was shaped by my early life experiences. I envy Christine's perpetual optimism and constant ability to instill hope in others who may not have identified a reason to feel hopeful. I have always believed that being aware of your weaknesses and what you want to change about yourself is the first step to transformation.

Despite Christine's optimism, she also readily admits that she and I share some of the same internal demons. We are constantly fighting the demons within us; the voices of self-doubt and insecurity, to find the positivity.

We cling to hope. Without hope, I am not sure I would be here today or have gotten where I am. It was hope that allowed me to take those big steps; get married, have a son, open a business, and run for a national office. It is hope that allows me to wake up every day and do what I do in caring for patients. I have hope that in my own little way I can make a difference in another person's life.

While I have admitted to you hope doesn't always come easy to me, I bet many would never know this. I give everything I have to remain positive, hopeful, and put a smile on my face even when I feel like I am dying on the inside. I also recognize that some of the hardest people for me to deal with are those who are perpetually negative. That personality type sucks the life out of me. I never want to be that person; the person who is draining to be around even when they have so much for which to be grateful. You see, I really believe that even in our darkest hours, there is always much for which to be grateful and to have hope!

One of the things that I have learned over the years is that it is hard to hope for things you don't even know exist.

Growing up as we did, Christine and I had no idea how big the world was, the experiences that would await. We hoped for a life that was easier than the one from which we came.

Over the years, I spent a lot of time talking with my mom about my life and her life with my dad. She and my dad were always the most positive people. No matter what circumstances they were dealt, they were always positive human beings. I often told Mom that I work as hard as I do to create a life for me and my family that is easier than the life she and my dad had. They always had to worry about money and unexpected bills, about having enough food, and making sure that we had oil in the tank to heat our home.

One day, my mother remarked "I would never want your life. It comes with too many commitments and too much responsibility." What an interesting perspective.

No matter how hard things are, it is important that we find some hope; hope for a better day than yesterday, a better life than our parents, a healthy family, or a simple vacation. Hope enables all of us to move forward, to put one foot in front of the other, and to take that risk. Christine and I are so blessed to have hope.

About You

At some point in life, every one of us asks, "Who Am I?"

It is our belief that asking the question is in itself an act of hope.

Change and evolving as a person is natural. Like waves that keep coming to shore and eroding the shoreline, hope lies in what the indomitable waves leave behind: beautiful gems of the sea, sea shells newly cast off by growing creatures, polished stones, smooth and unique, and beautiful, soft sand ready for our imprint as we walk forward. Just as each wave adds a bit of beauty to the beach, its ebb takes away the imprint we left ensuring that the prior moment is whisked into memory.

Questions for Self-Discovery and Thought

1. How do you stay in touch with, or get in touch with that core of Hope that is within each of us?

2. What have you done for yourself lately to nourish hope in yourself? In others?

3. Take five minutes each morning to start your day with journaling.

4. Identify something daily that gives you hope.

5. Name three things that you hope for.

6. Action is necessary for change. What can you do to make your hope a reality?

CHAPTER 2

Good People on Both Sides of the Tracks

Resilience

"the capacity to recover quickly from difficulties, toughness"

Wendy

TODAY I RETURNED TO MEREDITH, the town I called home for the first twenty years of my life. Having been away for so long, it is easy to see the town with a different lens. While much remains the same, more has changed since I left to attend college years ago. The asbestos mill, where my grandmother worked for thirty years before dying from an asbestos-related cancer when I was 13 years old, is now a beautiful hotel and shopping venue. The bowling alley, my Friday night hangout, is now the local dollar store.

Today, the physical changes really hit me. They seem profound. Maybe it is because I have not been here in years, or maybe it is because I see them with a lens of maturity and success; and more to the point perhaps, the lens of *I am really okay*.

My friends often speak fondly about going back home to see their elementary school or childhood home. I have never shared an emotional connection to my childhood home. Don't get me wrong; I have a lot of great memories. I had parents who sacrificed everything to make sure I had what I needed and to make sure that I was college educated. But returning home, for me, is difficult and not something I am ever excited to do. For me, returning home is a reminder of the past, a past that I have worked hard to survive and move beyond.

Today, as I drive up Parade Road and approach Smoky Hollow Trailer Park, I can see the grass is overgrown in front of our old mobile home. This is the grass my mother and father meticulously manicured. The new owners certainly don't take care of the lawn the way my parents did. The shrubs we planted when I was 10 years old are now so tall, they engulf the trailer. I can barely see the door.

I wonder, why would people let their home get this way? I can hear my mom's voice, so ingrained in my thoughts, "We may be poor, but we don't have to live like pigs or be dirty."

This is the home my parents were proud of. It cost $21,000 in 1976, and to them, it was a million-dollar home. It was better than either one of them had ever dreamed of owning.

As I glance to the other side of the road and the wide-open field, I remember a bright fall day when I was about 9 years old. It was six in the morning, the sun had risen, and my sister and I were getting ready for school. We were in my bedroom, located at the front of the trailer facing Parade Road.

I heard a loud bang. I recognized it as a gunshot. I knew this because my dad and I went deer hunting every fall, and I had shot a gun before. It was so close that Becky and I instinctively dropped to the floor to get out of sight. I peeked out my bedroom window and saw the elderly man, a recluse who lived across the street. He was standing at the side of the road with a gun pointed to his head. With the next bang, he fell to the ground. Although I couldn't fully process what was happening at the time, I knew he was no longer alive. My mom went running across the street to check on him while I held my sister and covered her face. No nine and six-year-old should have to witness or be party to such trauma. While my mom and dad worked with the police, I got my sister ready for school and we got onto the bus. We proceeded to school, like any other day.

This episode is my first recollection of a skill I have mastered, a mental toughness, which I believe is central to my professional and business successes. Resiliency!

Recently, one of my employees described me to another employee as tough, but fair. This childhood incident and numerous others throughout my life have made me tough. I learned, early in life, to partition off bad events and continue-on with the day, no matter how bad they seemed. For me, the ability to do this is critical to my survival, both personally and professionally. My lifelong motto has been to never let them see me sweat.

While many people may critique this approach and may argue that this doesn't allow me to grieve or process life events, I would argue that processing stressful life events isn't a cookbook recipe which follows an order. It is okay to individualize your stress and how you manage it. While everyone is different, the key to my resiliency is to compartmentalize the event and process it when I am mentally and physically able.

When bad or adverse events happen in my workday or in my personal life, I possess the ability to rapidly assess the situation, process it for acuity, and then move on to deal with all the issues which need to be addressed.

As a primary care provider to thousands of patients, there are days where I give people devastating and life-altering diagnoses. While giving these diagnoses rock me to the core internally, it is my job to make sure that the patient gets what is needed and that the next patient is unaware of what has happened prior to their visit. They need my full attention as well. Despite shaking on the inside and the overwhelming anxiety and fear, I must remain calm on the outside.

When I look at the business bank accounts and see them lower than they should be, I must set these thoughts aside until I have finished with my day. It is not for the employees to worry about.

As a professional speaker, when a text from an employee delivering their resignation comes in just before stepping on the stage, no matter how devastated and rocked to the core I am, the show must go on.

I am tough to the world. I am strong, articulate, driven, and a workhorse. All true. And equally true is that internally, I don't always feel that way. And that it is okay! I suspect I am not much different from you.

Women like me are often described by others as cold or heartless. For me, it couldn't be further from the truth. The difference is that my armor serves as my protector to allow me to survive and persevere. For years, I have felt badly about this trait. I have come to learn, that it is valuable and a trait that makes me a better clinician, businesswoman, employer, friend, and mother.

As a woman, you will deal with stressors every day. It is not what they are but how you deal with them that can make the difference, personally and professionally. Take the time to protect yourself and process events before responding. For me, it is the key to my survival, my resilience, and my success.

Christine

WHAT IS RESILIENCE? It's survival. It's withstanding, overcoming, and prevailing. But against what? The word itself implies it's fighting against something. Resilience stands against anything that threatens to defeat. Defeat what? You. Your soul. Your happiness. Anything that withdraws precious monies from the bank of your mental and physical health.

I am resilient. I am a person who has survived. Despite anguish, hurt, loss, despair, heartache that seemed debilitating and crushing, and too many hours on my knees praying for Gods help, I rose back up. That, too, is resilience: the ability to pull yourself out of the morass of despair to begin again.

I wish I could tell you how to avoid the hard things in life, how to take a course that protects you. Sadly, that is impossible. I can, however, share the techniques that helped me prevail against seemingly difficult odds. I don't think my story is unique, not really. I think I am the culmination of an aware and analyzed life comprised of incidents that are visible with great clarity in hindsight.

We continually overcome challenges. We grow past lessons that hurt. We move in and out of depressive states, changing mindsets brought to dark places by emotionally impacted actions.

I feel sad for people who lack the ability to feel strong emotion. I often think, *How unfortunate it is to see life with a gray lens.* I believe people who lack emotion walk through life dulled, experiencing a sensory deprivation, without even being aware of the lack.

As a person with heightened emotion, who interacts with the world, sensing everything in my peripheral view, I take great joy in connecting with humanity. I have always felt every emotion on an amplified level. I have had to learn, when the feeling is negative, to recover faster than I had in the past.

That said, I still carry with me today the deepest scars from my greatest heartaches, and those things changed me as well. The human soul is amazingly beautiful and amazingly resilient. We withstand events and circumstances that make us feel as though we are dying. We are tough at our core. We can withstand incredible blows and eventually overcome heartache.

I am certain that the word resilient represents my survival. Maintaining a resilient spirit brought me to where I am now, as if an invisible force came to save me in my most dire of places in life. I found myself hanging on for many years of my life, waiting for something greater. Along the way, I had to become resilient in a way that only people who are truly stubborn could completely understand.

One such instant of resilience was when I had to overcome clinical depression following a relationship break up. I did not see the slippery slope occurring as it played out. Day in and day out, I dwelled on my sadness. Thoughts haunted me daily. The stark reality of living alone suddenly evoked a true sadness that just cloaked my existence.

I began to sleep more. I began to wake later. I didn't want to dress. Eventually I found it difficult to shower. I would literally have to lie down in the shower, for long periods of time, to muster the energy to wash and then lay wet in my robe, unable to towel dry.

I didn't recognize what was happening to me then. I had a full commission job and was able to make my own hours, so I worked in bursts, accomplishing just enough to keep my income afloat and masking to the outside world the desperate spiral I found myself in. It would not be me that brought this to my attention. I slid so far down this slope that I was rescued by a coworker who suspected I was in trouble and knocked on my door until I opened it. He had been trained as a counselor, and he had recognized the signs I couldn't see myself. He stood at my door, and he shouted exactly the right words, "It doesn't matter to me how you look, just open the door."

I didn't want to answer the door. I knew how horrible I must look, but his words connected. It felt as if I was spending the last energy I could possibly muster as I lifted myself and took the final steps to open the door.

Even he was not prepared for what he saw but not surprised. He told me I needed to go to the hospital. And so, I went. Of course, I would be placed in the psychiatric ward of this hospital.

Even my time sense was warped. I felt like months had passed, when only a few weeks prior I had been a thriving, happy, active, and productive person.

As I lay that first night in my room, the nurse and doctors educated me about clinical depression. They provided papers to read to reinforce their words. I was made to move, to get up, to walk, to eat (something I had stopped doing).

I came to understand as I looked around, that I was not the only person battling demons.

It is amazing how the human mind protects the psyche. I had this internal debate going on, denying the very illness that brought me down. "Surely, I was not like these others here in this hospital. No, I was better, I was *more worthy and more successful. My life was nothing like these people, some who battled multiple illnesses."*

And yet, really, I was like them. Depression does not discriminate. Depression is an equal opportunity mental health condition. It affects the young, the old, the rich, the poor, and all races and ethnic groups.

The journey out of clinical depression saw my resilience tested. Resilience was the source I drew upon to take one more step when I could not see beyond it. I learned to not judge myself, to not look in the mirror in disdain. Resilience enabled me to accept and know that I was human and worthy; that I was like everyone else in the world.

For the first time, I acknowledged that I loved with all my heart, and the consequence would always be that my heart would be vulnerable to pain. I accepted that love was a mighty weapon that could bring me to my knees when I opened my heart up completely to the possibility of injury.

The journey to health took time, strength, hope and yes, resilience. Life took me to my knees, and I have always since keenly understood the power inherent in both the fall and the ability to rise again, with even greater strength and determination.

Resilience is not for the faint of heart.

It's not something people always win in the game of life.

I look back now and see that time in my life as a great lesson. Because of that fall, I have *kept it moving*. My enemy is *thinking* and *over thinking* in times of sadness or trauma.

All people have the capacity to dwell. I think true resilience is mastering one's ability to withstand both mental and physical pain and master the struggle to endure and overcome.

I have adapted a set of mechanics that function as life-saving actions for me. I live by the self-imposed rules shared here:

- Allow yourself to feel the pain of loss, heartache, or strife, whatever it might be, and then move on.
- Distract yourself by doing things to avoid dwelling.
- Be aware when you are dwelling.
- Be active and aware daily of your activities.
- Ask for help.
- Talk to friends, family, and professionals if need be.
- Take care of yourself. I work out, eat, and sleep according to regimens that are part of my daily life.
- Pray, read, and write. These activities are truly helpful.

I am now able to help others by sharing these tactics. While I am clearly not a therapist, as a professional coach, I do, on occasion, recognize similar plights in my students and clients. I am grateful to be able to give this advice. Perhaps now, after reading this, my clients, my friends, will know that I truly do understand.

About You

To fail is deeply human, as is the desire and ability to inspect, learn from, and transcend failure. Resilience is about getting through pain and disappointment without letting them crush your spirit. Accepting feelings of inadequacy and resisting the urge to judge oneself too harshly are critical skills to cultivate when it comes time to bouncing back from tough times.

What is it that resilient people do as they persist after missteps? Why is it that one person who loses a leg in an accident is unable to accept and grieve the loss, while another goes on national TV a few days after being attacked by a shark, demonstrating a resiliency that transcends belief? Ultimately, failures teach lessons beyond resilience. It is the lessons we chose to learn that allow us to grow and bounce back stronger than before.

Questions for Self-Discovery and Thought

1. How do you handle personal and professional setbacks?

2. Do you demand perfection from yourself? From others?

3. Are you able to accept a mix of losses and wins?

Research shows that resilience is a trait that can be enhanced and learned. Here is a brief checklist of suggestions for improving your own ability to be resilient:

- Don't react. Take time to think and process before engaging.
- Sleep on it. Most events are more easily processed the next day.
- Practice responding to various situations. Sometimes working out possibilities in your mind before an event occurs allows for a planned response.
- Build positive beliefs in your abilities. It's okay to tell yourself that you are smart, resilient, kind, or whatever positive adjective describes you and that you believe!
- Develop a strong social network
- Embrace change. Change is inevitable. When you find a way to embrace it and challenge yourself, the reward is self-confidence.
- Nurture yourself
- Establish goals and take action

CHAPTER 3

Making Friends

Idealism

"unrealistically aiming for perfection"

Wendy

WHEN YOU HEAR THE WORD IDEALISTIC, it may conjure up a negative connotation. Do you think, "She is idealistic, she doesn't have a handle on reality. She just doesn't get it." Some people do. But for me personally, I don't think it is bad to be idealistic if it is balanced with a healthy piece of reality.

I have often seen social media posts that say something like, "I hope your life is as good as you make it appear on Facebook." Desiring a great marriage, a rewarding career, or a happy and healthy family is certainly idealistic, but I don't think there is anything wrong with it. I believe that aspiring for the ideal is what pushes us all. It is certainly what keeps me moving forward and putting one foot in front of the other. It is what makes me get up and go to work every day, even on those days when I don't think I can possibly do it.

Why is it bad to be so idealistic that you want this world to be a better place where children are safe from school shootings? Why is it idealistic or bad to expect that our kids have food on their plates and healthcare when they are ill? Without principles and striving for the ideal, this country would not be where it is today.

Our work is not done. We still have so much work to do to make this country a better place. I maintain that alone, we do less, but together, we can do so much more.

For as long as I can remember, I have been a perfectionist; my mom and dad, even more so. I remember my dad telling me, "If you are going to do something, don't just do it *half-ass,* do it well."

He would sit for hours to help me with a school project or science exhibit, even when I had long since moved on from the task. He would remind me that everything I put out personally or professionally is a reflection of me and who I am.

To this day, I have not forgotten his messages. When I think about cutting a corner to move things along or get more tasks accomplished, I can't do it. I bring to the table everything I have with every task I accept; even when no one is watching or judging. I won't accept mediocrity in myself.

My parents instilled that quality in both of their daughters. Becky (my sister) and I will work seven days per week if it means the difference between just doing something and doing it well.

As a nurse practitioner working in an MD-owned clinic, I became increasingly disenchanted with my work. The pressures to see more people and return more calls were mounting yet the incentives and pay were not. I found myself unable to put my head on the pillow at night and know that I had given the best care possible. I was struggling to stay afloat.

You see, I believe to my core that every patient I see deserves to have the best of me, and I wasn't able to live up to my own moral compass. They didn't deserve to have limited time with me because the pressures of the healthcare system made spending time with them nearly impossible.

Is this idealistic? I would say it absolutely is and my patients deserve nothing less.

After weeks of agonizing over my future, I made the decision to resign my clinical practice. It was time to do some self-reflection and figure out where I wanted to spend the next twenty-five years of my career. Little did I know that closing that window opened the biggest door of my career.

This decision led to the opening of two-family practices and provided me the ability to create a place where patients are given the care and the time they deserve. Striving for the ideal while confronting reality, single-handedly transformed my career and hopefully the career of the eight nurse practitioners who work alongside me every day.

In 2013 and 2014, I served as the Co-chair and Chair for our national nurse practitioner clinical conference. It was a large task involving more than 1,000 speakers and 5,000 attendees. The planning began a year before the meeting. By all accounts, the conference was an overwhelming success. It was the highest grossing meeting the organization had produced to date.

Leading up to the meeting, I announced that I was incredibly honored for having been given the chance to serve in this capacity, but that I would not continue as Chair, if asked, after the meeting was over. Many expressed that they were shocked that I would walk away in the shadow of such a successful meeting.

To me, it was simple. For two years, I gave the organization every ounce of energy I had (it was a volunteer position). I had biweekly meetings every week to plan the conferences. It was such an honor to be asked, but to keep up this time commitment while speaking, running my practices, and seeing patients was overwhelming and was starting to fatigue me physically and emotionally. For me, it was better to go out on top, loving every minute of what we had accomplished, than to spend the next year giving it less than it deserved. I never wanted to give this conference and my colleagues anything less than my all. It was one of the hardest decisions I have made, to walk away from something I loved so much. However, it was the right thing to do for the organization.

So yes, I would tell you I am an idealist. I expect perfection from myself and others around me. I am also, however, a realist. I recognize that none of us are perfect. Yet, it should not stop us from trying! Our patients, families, colleagues, and children deserve it.

Christine

TONIGHT, WILL BE MY LAST night sleeping in this house. My Mom and Dad have saved their precious monies, worked their butts off and have purchased a new trailer for us. I am so excited. I know my parents are excited, too as we took a ride after dinner to go look at the new place. Flashlights in hand, the trailer arriving from far away and was custom built for us. Everything chosen, our colors, counter tops, cupboards, we can't wait. This means no more sharing of one room for us three girls. My older sister, Tammy will get her own room with a bathroom of her very own. My younger sister Heidi and I will share another room. Proof that hard work pays, we are so very lucky and just in time for my tenth birthday. Things are certainly looking up for us.

In order to truly feel happy, I had to live within the bubble I created. My parents worked hard. Really hard. They didn't choose their own upbringing. They had made their own mishaps along the way, having us children at a very young age, but they endured. They stuck together as a team. They cleaned everything to the bone. A speck of dust would die of loneliness in our house. We could eat off the floors. We didn't wear shoes in our house, nor did a single article of clothing sit inside a drawer sloppy, no, our clothes were stacked in perfect folded stacks, inside the drawers, subject to inspection. If the drawers were sloppy, they would get dumped onto our beds and we would have to refold and replace the articles and gain approval for the replacement of the drawer back into its slot in our bureaus. Our economical standard did not define our cleanliness. Where anyone thought poverty and dirt resided in the same places haven't really been in the hoods where that can be proven untrue.

Many of the most wretched external homes have the cleanest interior environments, proving, in its cliché how you can't judge a book by its cover. We were living proof of that.

Our new home would get delivered and we would get to decorating it and it was quite beautiful. People would come visit us and they would all say how it didn't even feel like a trailer inside, and it didn't. When you were inside our home, it was quite pleasant for visitors. For sleep over guests alike. My family had family who would come visit us frequently, and us girls had many friends. It was the place I would have my sweet sixteen birthday party.

This milestone in our lives I know did not come easy for my parents and maybe this is where the lessons in my life began. Maybe this is where my example in life was set. My parents weren't big on long lectures, life lessons or speeches. Our lessons were learned from watching, not talking. I was the talker, born with a gift to gab, feeling early on, I had a lot to say, a lot to share and I noticed that people listened. I can see looking back, that the lessons my parents bestowed on me were going to be additions to a story untold, that through my lens, through my mouth and my mind, would come the sharing of the incredible journey me and my family took from where we started to now. This is as much their story as it is mine. They, too evolved and god knows without their hard work, I would not have survived in a safe, warm and loving environment, albeit poor. Poor by societal standards, rich by moral standards.

When I thought about what I wanted to be when I grew up, I didn't let myself dream an impossible dream, I knew that even though I aspired to be something amazing and something big, that right now I had to focus on the ground in front of me and move, that I needed to take steps every day and I innately woke each day invigorated as if God had planted an internal seed in my brain from the start that constantly told me I was running out of time. I have often felt that I have lived many lives already.

As I write this, I already know I've seen parts of the world that people will never see, that I've done amazing things, that I have earned amazing opportunities that gave me large podiums to speak my story out loud for stranger filled audiences who loved my words spoken and that has been liberating. As if, unafraid, I know that what I have experienced and what I have done is not unlike every single American story. That we all have this amazing struggle to triumph over the harsh realities around us. I feel like sometimes it's obvious that the good in this world is certainly now outweighed by the evil, brought on my men (and by men, I mean humankind not gender.) We have such horror around us at times, I wonder how so many people could be so far off course from the obvious path we were all meant to walk.

When did it become so unpopular to work hard and so easy to do nothing? Why did so many parents before us allow their kids to be spoiled? In hindsight, I think that many kids I was surrounded by had luxury brought on by their parents' wealth. Those kids became comfortable with that lifestyle.

Unfortunately, that was not the case for me. I learned early on I had to work for what I wanted and that everything required hard work. I think a sense of entitlement for many generations has caused a ton of societal issues. There is a lost generation of hardworking, old-school work ethic. It began in our era and time, but because of our economic environment, Wendy and I are an example of its continuance—by exception and circumstance but not the rule.

Here we are, so is my story special anymore? I think it is. Not because I fool myself into believing that I am extraordinary, although I am constantly written about that I am, in my profession, an exception. But what about me, the human?

Am I special, is my story special? Yes. Overcoming odds is a special story. Not unique. Not elite. Not rare. But special yes. Because too many of my peers will not stand up to say what they need to for themselves. Won't put the time and work ethic into building a life that is difficult but hugely rewarding. So many people do not even know what they are living for, their purpose, unknown and not even thought of, aimlessly living lives, using our worldly resources, eating, playing, vacationing, and by much smaller percentages you find the philanthropists, the charitable folk, the educators, movers and shakers. They exist, but they do not outnumber those taking and not replacing the same goods and things built and made by the other percentage of people trying to push a million-pound boulder up a growing mountain.

So, I digress. Coming back to my full circle point, Idealism, Ideology, being Idealistic is a gift. But I do believe people can hone skills that make them look for the silver lining in all things. Like working out your muscles at the gym, you need to train. You need to be self-aware, able to control your mind and thoughts, which is also a trick. We often, as humans, follow our mind. We don't realize our mind is a muscle in a body and we are the captain of that ship. But we are. We control where our mind leads us, by making thoughtful choices in what we choose to watch on tv, what we tune into music wise, what we read, who we engage with and talk to, who we choose for friends. Life and our minds are about good choice making. #makeagood-choice #choosewisely

I guess what I want to leave you with here in this section is the ideology that happiness and contentment, even success, can't come from money. It can only come from being free to be your very best self.

My parents were wired to give me that. To hold us accountable in the hardest ways. It seemed cruel when it was happening and by today's standards probably would be a crime, not to imply abuse, but moreover to imply how soft we've become as a society.

There is a reason as an animal we need training. As a human-kind we need discipline. Self-discipline and external discipline. My parents gave me the greatest tools, gifts, and lessons money could buy, by example, by setting house rules that were standards we lived or died by. They gave me my life barometer and as such they gave me the ability to dream, to have an idea of the idealistic world I wanted to live in or create.

I have veered from that path more than once, only to find how right those barometers were. We all need bumpers on life, that keep us from falling into the gutters. What are your bumpers? Do you have any? Will you know when you are veering off the path? These are all human questions that we must as people understand the answers to personally. Mistakes will happen. How you correct course will be what is written about in your legacy.

About You

Perhaps being an idealist is like being a little bit pregnant. You either are or you aren't; it's not possible to be a little bit idealistic. What is possible is to embrace and find value in striving for idealism while embracing the practical aspects of living and working in the real world. Idealism is a state of mind that is brought to life by having ideals and living within their scope.

Questions for Self-Discovery and Thought

1. Do you have a story from your youth that illustrates the difference between the reality of the time and an idealistic memory?

2. Do you think being idealistic is a positive or negative trait?

   Think about and explore why you believe this way. Journal about how this belief impacts you and your interactions with others.

3. Do you think being idealistic has helped you in your life personally and professionally?

    If yes, why? If no, why not?

CHAPTER 4

Those Not at the Table
Are on the Menu

Strategy

"carefully designed or planned to serve a purpose or advantage"

Wendy

SOME OF MY EARLIEST CHILDHOOD MEMORIES
include shopping for school clothes with my mom and
dad. From as early as 5 or 6 years of age, I remember
looking forward to this annual August tradition. We spent
days traversing the state looking for just the right outfits.
The dresses, hair accessories, tights, and shoes all had to
be perfect and coordinate.

While this annual shopping adventure was certainly
designed to get clothing for the upcoming New Hampshire
winters; it was also to find that perfect first day of school

outfit. This time was exciting and fun for me and my mom; not so much for my sister and dad. They reluctantly endured the hours of shopping. This was just not their thing.

When I found that perfect first day of school outfit, I knew it and so did my mom. Her face would light up with pride as I walked out of the fitting room. She was as excited as I was about our find.

While there was not a lot of money in our home, every outfit I got from the discounted stores was perfect and portrayed the type of look that my parents desired for me. Despite the limited money, each year my clothes reflected the latest trend and look. This became increasingly difficult as I got older, and the clothes became more expensive.

As I approached my teen years, it became important to me to have name-brand clothing. The Jordache Jeans, the Laura Ashley and Gunny Sack dresses, and the Dickie pants were all brands I desired. When I was 12 years old, my dad informed me that it was time to get a job if I wanted to have this kind of clothing.

It didn't take me long to find a job. I applied for and was hired at a local arcade and driving range. I would get up every morning at five am and ride my bike, along with Christine, to my job about three miles away.

There I would pick up golf balls for $1.00 per bucket and all the arcade tokens that I could carry. On any given morning, I would make $10.00–$15.00 dollars cash. I would save this money all summer for our annual shopping trip. By pooling my money with my parents, I could have the clothes I wanted, the clothes I felt that I needed to fit in.

Every evening, my mom and I would strategically pick out my clothes to wear to school the next day. Once chosen, I would settle in for the night, and my mother would then spend hours meticulously ironing every piece of clothing. She would get me up for school at least two hours before school began each morning to allow me time to shower. This also gave her time to make sure my hair and clothes were just right. It was important to my mom that my sister and I were always clean and well-dressed.

Why? Why was our appearance so important to my mother? Neither of my parents grew up wealthy. In fact, they were quite poor. Neither completed high school. My mom was 18 years old when she married my father, an Air Force veteran. My mother's childhood home was a tar-paper shack with an outhouse for a bathroom. There were times she lacked running water.

Despite her poverty, she would get up each morning and meticulously get herself ready for school. She ironed her clothes every day and made sure her hair was perfectly coifed. She often told me that she fit in throughout her school years because of her appearance. She credited her cleanliness and well-maintained appearance with her teachers giving her opportunities that others, from the same social class, were not given. She believed that first impressions mattered and that one's appearance can and will cost them opportunities.

My sophomore year in college, I took a sociology class. For my class project, I decided to put my mother's theory to the test. Do people judge you based upon your appearance? Your clothes? Your cleanliness? I took the subway in Boston to Chestnut Hill, an affluent suburb of Boston. I wore jeans and a wrinkled sweatshirt. My hair was a mess, and I had on no makeup. I walked into Bloomingdale and not one person, over the course of 30 minutes, asked to help or assist me. I was invisible.

I took the subway back to my dormitory, changed my clothing and put on a suit. I applied make-up, curled my hair and proceeded back to the store. The same sales associates were still working the floor. Within 30 seconds of walking in, I was asked if I needed assistance.

I remember thinking, *I looked worthy of their attention. I was no longer invisible.*

I asked one associate, "Do you remember me, I was here one hour ago?"

Of course, the answer was, "I am sorry but, no."

I know my story is not unique. Many of you may have had a similar encounter. This type of invisibility occurs every day in our country and is often based upon race, ethnicity, age, or gender. This project burned an impression in my brain that continues to affect me today. While I would like to say that I have done a lot of ground-breaking work to correct these wrongs of society, unfortunately, I have not.

These impressions and life lessons are with me every day in my professional career. In college and graduate school, I got up every morning, showered, fixed my hair, and put on makeup. I wore professional clothing to class every day. While none of my clothes were expensive by today's standards, they were professional. I believe that when you dress for success, you will be successful. When you feel good about yourself, you portray confidence.

I also believe that dressing this way made me stand out in a room of others who didn't. I credit this with a lot of the success I had in both my undergraduate and graduate school career. Numerous faculty members took me under their wing and gave me opportunities that I don't believe I would have otherwise had. A few of my graduate faculty, who have become my friends, still speak about how I was always dressed professionally and ready to learn. In my opinion, it cast a positive first impression that today, thirty years later, they still remember.

Today, I choose my clothes for each upcoming professional engagement. Whether I am speaking to a room of 10,000 nurse practitioners or five CEOs, I strategically choose my clothes, my hair and make-up to convey the message I am there to deliver. I have learned, just like my mom, that it is often not what you say but how you look and appear that creates this first impression. When I consult with others interested in pursuing a professional speaking career, I emphasize that it is often not what you say but how you carry yourself and how you appear which casts that first impression. Negative first impressions are often hard to overcome.

When hiring employees for my companies, it should be noted that first impressions matter. One potential candidate showed up for her interview chewing gum. When I introduced myself to her, she took the gum out of her mouth, put it between her fingers, and proceeded to shake my hand with the gum tucked in between her fingers. Another potential employee showed up for a professional job interview wearing clothes that looked as if she had just climbed out of bed.

I asked myself, *will she be conscientious with my business when she does not seem to care about her appearance? Will she be comprehensive in caring for my patients when she clearly wasn't thoughtful with this presentation?*

The first impression I formed of these women would be the first impression a customer has of my business. I want to say the same standards apply to men, yet I am not convinced that they are held to the same standards.

In summary, be strategic daily. Choose to make those positive first impressions. You never know when that positive impression will transform your career.

The first impressions I make have given me advantages over others. It is important to know that you don't need expensive clothing or jewelry. Take time to dress for the role and the image you wish to portray. You will be amazed at the opportunities that come your way.

Christine

IF I HAD TO WRITE THE TOP FIVE things I remember about Wendy and her sister Becky as little girls, number one would be their clothing. They were always dressed impeccably. I can remember being in their home and always seeing how incredibly neat Carol, Wendy's mom, was with the folding and ironing of their clothes. There was always an ironing board set up. Their clothes were pressed, and the girls looked amazing; from the first day of kindergarten when Becky and I went off to Lang Street School and all throughout their many years to high school graduation.

As a professional woman today, I mirror Wendy's sentiment. I also think about how incredible it is that we somehow were given the opportunity to wear nice clothing because of sacrifices our parents made for us. I also have this incredible admiration for our parents for having the mindset to teach us such valuable lessons in our lives.

Then still, when I really stop and think beyond my own journey and Wendy's I can recall on photos of my parents and know that this was something that they didn't have the luxury of themselves and so it dawns on me just now writing these very words, that while I knew they did not have much growing up and they still sacrificed beyond their childhoods to cloth us, that they never complained about it.

Isn't that an incredible thing? They **broke a cycle** of poverty in the specific area of our dress, our first impressions, as Wendy so eloquently states, and they did that with extreme class, dignity, and humbleness.

Like Wendy's mother, my mother took great care to get us nice clothing. I would tell you Wendy and Becky were the envy of our entire school with their clothing, so while my parents ensured we always had new school clothes and pretty clothes, we weren't wearing the top name brands at our house. Still, if you look at my clothing in my little girl photos, you will see I was wearing pretty clothing and I can recall it making such an impression on me that it had been as impressionable on me as key moments in my life. As I write this and recall upon my childhood clothing, I can recall what I wore my very first day of school. I can recall the blue and orange stitching in the cute top and I also recall a favorite t-shirt that had a boy and girl kissing on the front. I wore it all the time and if my mother had not asked me to change my clothes, I may have worn it every day. So, as you can see, as a person of lesser means, I still cared deeply about my presentation and I still know my parents cared about it as well. It was important and I would argue clothing was a very important thing that was antiquated with stature, or acceptance and in our school even more so. I am grateful we met the bill and yet I do know that my own contributions from summer jobs helped me find my way to the name brand stores where even more acceptance could be doled out by way of helping me fit in rather than stand out for the wrong reasons. Sometimes strategy is more about not striking a different path or differentiation. I understood what it meant to be different for the wrong reasons.

I think I carried that strategy with me for many decades where I understood the need to be a chameleon of my environment. When I grew to be a young adult, and I was dating a man of greater financial stature, there were many firsts I would experience at an age that probably would have come to others far earlier in life. I was careful not to expose that about myself.

My senior class trip was one of those times when others had flown to vacation destinations and for me it was my first trip on a plane. Instead of spending the day at Disney World where I would have loved to see the entire park, the girls I was with wanted to take the train off the park campus and go lay by a pool and tan for the day, having been there many times prior. I went along but was internally disappointed that there I was at Disney World for the first time and wouldn't even see it. When I reflect today at the price tag I paid to fit in, it adds up quickly. But that strategy would bode me well in life and business later, because few people came equipped as I did for survival. I could morph into any scenario and hold a poker face. When others would complain and moan about things, I endured with no reaction. I had learned long ago to hold my proverbial breath and often that would help me compete and win when competing.

I can remember where I was when I ate at my first true restaurant. I was with a girlfriend for a sleepover and I was fourteen. When I say eat a real restaurant, I mean one that wasn't fast food. I mean a real sit-down place with a menu. I remember thinking I had no clue what I was doing. I wondered if anyone would know. Thankfully, the family would order for us as it was a Chinese restaurant, and I was saved as I sat there looking at the menu in dismay. Yet, the drink I had, my first Shirley Temple drink and the food would be the most amazing thing and I would sit there realizing how incredibly incredible the world was and how I knew so little about this world. I was struck by how I truly was not prepared to be in this big world with so little experience and I would question how I would be prepared to go out and survive.

As I write this, I am on the heels of holding my first industry convention for more than two hundred C suite executives in the banking industry at a Marriott with a food bill in the tens of thousands of dollars. My, how far I have come. Beyond my wildest dreams. Yes, now I am ordering food for the affluent for several meals in a set of days as my guest for my own convention. I am a long, long way from Parade Road now. And yet, I am still that little girl from the trailer park inside. I am the person who doesn't look down on people, who is amazed at the world and still discovering. I am strategic though, and if I had not been, I would not be where I am right now.

Strategy has carried me all the way to here. And will carry me beyond. I would tell you that today I coached someone who was in dismay of their employers pay for them. This person felt like they were being shorted and they felt their employer knew this to be the case. My answer was of course to prepare them to reset the meeting and to approach in an unemotional way. That said, I thought of the strategy of this intersection, which is hard-wired in my head with these scenarios. I knew that this woman was upset and that it's likely her employer senses her readiness to go to battle on her pay. I told her to do extra good at her job and to be exaggerative without being condescending, or patronizing about her love for her work, so they knew her goal was to save her job, not end it and to reach a resolution not the opposite. Life is as much about strategy as anything. I am not a seasoned strategist. It has come to me from surviving.

About You

The values we gain in childhood DO carry over into adulthood. Did our parents sit at night and plan strategies for parenting? Given who they are and the times we were raised in, it is more likely that they simply brought together, through love and a desire that their children have more than they, the best tools and tips they could gather.

The concept of dress for success is not new. People do judge others by their appearance. Our parents knew this from experience, from harsh and painful lessons learned. They hoped to spare us those same lessons, and in this one area, they were successful. There were plenty of other painful lessons for us, but we are today impressive women who know how to make great first impressions—and beyond.

Questions for Self-Discovery and Thought

1. Are you strategic in your life? Plan for success, not failure.

2. First impressions matter and are often hard to overcome. Ask a trusted person to share their first impressions of you. Is there anything you would change after learning their thoughts?

3. Dress for success! When you feel good about yourself, you will achieve more. Create a positive first impression, you never know when your paths will cross again.

CHAPTER 5

No Place Lke Home

Focus, Drive

"relentlessly compelled by the need to accomplish goals, hard-working and ambitious"

Christine

WHAT DRIVES PEOPLE? THIS QUESTION is the topic of one of the biggest trends of current times, discovering your why.

I recently watched a YouTube video of Simon Sinek's TedX talk exploring the topic of his best-selling books, *Start with Why* and *Find Your Why*. I was struck by his statement that the core of finding your life's purpose is tying that passion to your profession or cause.

"People don't buy what you do, they buy WHY you do it." His words continued to resonate as he expanded that thought to say, when a person's drive flows from their why, they are living in their authentic self and can live in their truth and thus are passionate about living in that truth.

This is not a new concept to me. Herein lies the entire topic at hand. How does one's drive and focus manifest? If it's living in your WHY, then I hit the jackpot in life. I have been driving to my passion all my life.

As a little girl, I had this *think outside the box* mentality. I recall my kindergarten teacher, putting up a piece of drawn art on the chalk board and asking us to trace the picture. We all got copies of the art, and we laid our blank piece of paper over that drawing and we traced to the best of our 6-year-old capabilities.

I noticed at the bottom was my teacher's messy signature. In the place where our names were to be written, she had signed hers. I thought about it and decided she must want me to trace her signature, too. When I handed in my drawing amongst the twenty some odd kids in my class, no one but me had traced her signature.

When my mother came to pick me up that day, I vividly recall my teacher saying, "Mrs. Stiles, your daughter is bright. I want to show you what she did today."

They walked to my picture hanging on the wall, complete with the traced signature. I remember my mother smiled as the teacher said, "Christine is special."

This was the first time I heard those words. I beamed as I sat and listened to this exchange.

On the ride home, I thought about what the teacher had said, and I thought it was nice of her to call me special instead of scolding me or correcting me for doing the assignment wrong.

Today, I understand how that could have gone a different way. My teacher's name was Mrs. Yutz. She was a young woman, a new teacher, and popular teacher with an amazing bedside manner. She taught me two lessons that day.

1. Elevating people is important and easy to do. I learned that while it is easier to tear someone down, it is better and worth the effort to elevate instead.
2. When you accept people for their contributions and efforts instead of being critical of the details, both of you win.

I often wonder, why am I driven and focused? Why do I see life for its glory? Why do I see people for who they are as individuals? I don't know the answer. What I do know is that understanding this truth is a gift; an unbelievable, free, liberating and glorious gift. It's a gift to live peacefully aware of the beauty of life. It is a gift to see the world as special. It is a gift to see people as glorious— for all their faults, weaknesses, and imperfections.

Society wants to paint us with colors, separate us by age, by gender, by race. Yet the truth is that no matter our race, or our sexuality, our economic status, or religious beliefs, no one of us is better than another. There is no hierarchy but the imperfect societal rules we submit to.

I see strength in the most unsavory of people. I see love in the hardest of people. I see light in the most closed off person. I see beauty beyond skin, I see love beyond words, I see struggle beyond admission of it. I feel people. I connect with people. I never tire of life. Every day I wake with excitement. What amazing thing will today bring?

My drive comes from a desire to heal, help, lift, elevate, perpetuate, overcome and defend all that is good in this world. My goal is to draw the same out of people; to shine a light on the gifts all around us and within us. I feel it is my calling.

When I was poor as a child, I was happy, and healthy. And I also spent many days and nights crying for the injustice of not getting a birthday invitation; for not being able to buy a present for someone., for not being able to join a club that cost money at school, for having to wear something that others deemed less or inappropriate.

I don't blame the rich kids for their cruel treatment because they thought I was less deserving than them. I blame the world for creating a society where this is okay. Children are taught to segregate. They see the pecking order of monetary segregation, and they see what society rejects or amplifies. I know that I've been laughed at. I dreamed and shared my dreams when my dreams were ridiculous.

And yet, in my world, I have never felt deprived. In our house, we were clean. My mother was a neat freak. Every night we had warm, cooked meals. We sat around the table and shared stories from our day. We prayed. We were rich in many ways.

Somewhere inside me, I had a burning desire to write. A prolific calling at ages 7, 8 and 9, I spent days upon days scribbling poetry (that I still have today) into emotional rants that released closely held hurt into the universe, as if the very writing of the words was like blowing on a snow-white dandelion, sending seedling wishes into the air. My words freed me. My words saved me.

Today, I teach others (who suffer in their own way) how to be their best. When I am asked how to increase drive and focus, the answer comes back, always, to exploring and getting clear and strong in their personal place.

I have taken wrong roads, been distracted and traveled for long periods of time down roads that were mirages. I have been motivated by emotional pulling that had sinful attractions, without consciously recognizing it; trapped sometimes in a spell.

How do I help others avoid those dead-end roads I traveled? I can't. I can only help them recognize when they are on that same path and help them set a course that steers them back to the place where their consciousness can be whole and healthy.

It takes a soul that self-recognizes. The human brain is a machine that can work against the heart and soul; the human body, too. The brain and the body can drive you towards sinful desires, sinful habits, sinful places, people, and things.

The heart is your GPS. Your soul is the map. You must align the three: heart, body and soul.

There is a reason I believe that *body* is sandwiched between the heart and soul. Capture your body between your heart and soul and it will stay on the correct path. To do this, you must elevate your GPS and your map, and let those two steer the course and guide you to the right road. Only then can you live in true happiness.

I still have drive. I still work hard. I still know the clock is ticking in my ear, and I have much I want to do; much I want to see! I will do it. I will go. I will travel, and I will inhale life in all its adventures. I will drive to affect the best positive change I can.

Today I am living in my truth, my *WHY*.

I hope in sharing my story, others can figure out what their drive and focus is; that they, too, will learn to harness what is burning inside them.

Wendy

THE EARLIEST MEMORY I HAVE is from around the age of two. Maybe I remember it because it was repeatedly captured in the Polaroid pictures my mom and dad took, or maybe it is because it continues to reflect the person I am today.

> *I am eighteen months old, and Mom and I are sitting at the coffee table in our mobile home doing math problems. She crafts the four column addition problems, and I sit for hours to solve them. When I finished, I wait, impatient for her to grade my work. Using colored crayons, she marks the items correct with a big C or wrong with an X. I am excited to see her correct my work, write 100% in red, and place a sticker on the paper.*

To me, there was no better feeling; that feeling of success and satisfaction. If something was wrong with my work, I would sit there until I achieved a hundred percent grade. Even at that age, anything less than one hundred percent was unacceptable.

While this might seem strange or unusual, my mom was 18 years old when she gave birth to me. She had dropped out of high school to marry my dad. I honestly believe she knew that the only way for me to rise above our circumstances was to obtain an education, and she was driven to help me get it. She always told me that she knew I was smart and destined for great things from the day I was born and that nothing I ever accomplished surprised her.

I remember asking her once, "How did you know that I was smart?"

Her response, "Because the minute you were born, I said your name, and you looked at me like you understood. You always wanted to learn and were driven to be successful."

While I am a firm believer that intelligence and IQ are important, I am also a believer that we can all make up for some of our shortcomings with drive and determination. From a young age, I was determined to be the best student, the best musician, the most well-behaved, and to make all A's on my report card.

Today, I am driven by much of the same—to be the best mom, the best boss, or the best nurse practitioner that I can be. I have no idea what ticks inside of me, but all I know is that every single day, I am driven to be better than I am today.

Hard work, change, or new concepts don't scare me. What scares me is failure; failure at something that is important to me. I also believe that while I am never going to be the most brilliant or the most beautiful person in any room (it is okay to be honest), I can outwork anyone with my drive if it is something that interests and is important to me.

It is funny to me when people come up to me and say, "How do you do it all?"

My response is always, "I don't."

To the outside, I may seem to have it together with all that I do. However, what I have learned is that I can't do it all, and I need to stop feeling guilty for it. I have convened a village of people to enable to me to focus on my strengths and interests while leaving other tasks (which I don't enjoy or don't need to do myself) to those who do them better than I.

I am driven to be the best I can be at the things that are important to me; my family, my relationships, and my work. I can also honestly say that the things which are not important to me, such as cooking, are left to others who can do them better.

Women have lived their lives feeling guilty about not having the cleanest house, not being the best mom, or not being the perfect size. I have vowed to **break that cycle** of guilt. Is it easy? No, it most certainly is not, but recognizing that it exists is 99% of the battle.

My understanding husband of thirty-one years grew up in a home with a mom who was a fabulous cook. When he married me, I promptly let him know that I reviewed my marriage contract and the vows we took, and nowhere in there did it mention the need to cook. Therefore, he should not expect it. Thank goodness, he is forgiving of my shortcomings and recognizes my strengths.

While I know that at some time in history, it was declared that women *can have it all,* I don't believe we can have it all. Sacrifices and choices must be made.

I know for me that I cannot do it all and do it well. Anyone who can, I would love to meet them. As my friend Sharon once proclaimed, "You can only be good in one room of the house anyway, why make it the kitchen?"

So, for those of you feeling guilty about the things you don't do or do as well as others, let it go. If they are important to you, then use your drive to enhance your strengths. If they are not, stop feeling guilty for your shortcomings. Guilt just consumes your energies and saps your drive. But, like everyone reading this, I am challenged by this every single day and continue to be a work in progress.

In 2006, I left a family practice as an employee and opened my own primary care clinic. To open, I mortgaged our residential home to afford the start-up costs. There is nothing that makes you more motivated and driven to succeed than fear and worry that all you had worked for and built up in your family home and equity could be gone in the blink of an eye.

The day we opened, I had seven patients on the schedule with another one hundred or so committed to coming to the clinic but not yet booked. I wasn't sure how we were going to make it. I worked tirelessly, whatever it took; to make sure that the commitments I made to our staff (to provide them a paycheck) and to my family, were fulfilled.

Today, we have twenty-one employees and almost 6,000 patients. Did I fail or make mistakes? Yes, every day. But I was driven to be better and not make that same mistake again. I was willing to put in the time and do whatever it took to see this business succeed. I credit that drive (along with the best employees ever) with our success.

Three years ago, I decided to return to school for my doctorate. It was something I had wanted to do for such a long time, but there was never a good time to commit to the rigors of the program and all that would come with it.

During my last year, one of my courses was focused on leadership. For an assignment, we were required to read a book that has been transformational for me. The book was *Strength Finders 2.0* by Tom Rath.

Reading about my top five strengths was like reading my autobiography. It was eerie to me that a one-hour test could capture the essence of my personality and my whole life. As I had always known, my biggest strengths are drive and determination. However, I also learned something that I think is important to share.

Nowhere in this book did it discuss my weaknesses.

I have spent my life, like many of you, trying to improve my weaknesses; trying to insert a round screw in a square hole. All of this has left me drained, feeling guilty, and with less time to work on my strengths.

My epiphany, after reading that book, was to learn that it is okay to just be okay at the things in life that are not meaningful or important to the overall structure of life.

By coming to terms with this, I have been able to focus on the things in my life that have brought me success (personally and professionally) and let go of those things that I am never going to change.

When people ask me where my drive comes from, if I am to be honest with you, it is likely the result of my genetic predisposition (while my mom and dad were not driven by their own education or professional success, they were driven by their desire to see their kid's succeed) and shaped by my environment.

Since I was a little girl, I have always needed to have a safety net; a savings account that could support me, extra food in the pantry, or extra supplies in the home (yes, Sam's and BJ's are where my husband and I spend date night). This is likely because I worried constantly as a child about not having enough of these. I vowed as an adult to make sure I didn't worry about these again. I frequently tell my husband that I am driven by my need to NOT worry about such things. For me, this worry consumes too much of my energy. I would rather work nonstop to make sure I have my little safety net than to live by the seat of my pants and worry every day.

Drive does not always equate with success. Most recently, I ran for a national office in my NP organization and I wasn't successful. I lost to a worthy and amazing opponent. However, that didn't stop the sadness, the feelings that maybe I am not worthy, or the deprecating self-talk. Although I took a few days to feel sorry for myself, I dug deep and began to navigate my plans for the next challenge.

Life is going to throw us all curves. Life doesn't always go how we plan or envision. Mine certainly has not. However, to me, drive and being driven means the difference between navigating my own life or letting others do it for me. I chose the latter. My drive has enabled me to navigate my own ship, even if it's only a dinghy. That, to me, is success.

About You

No surprise that Drive and Focus are words that resonate deeply with us. There is a reason we've paired these words. True greatness can only be accomplished when we are able to focus all our attention on what we're doing at the moment. Drive is about momentum and direction. Focus is about getting the job done. The sun beam can produce a flame when it is focused and not when it isn't.

Questions for Self-Discovery and Thought

1. What drives you? Are you driven by your own needs, or are you driven by the needs of others?

2. Make a list of words that best describe you. Then read Strength Finders and review your strengths. See if they match, and if not, think about why. Were you honest in your own assessment of your strengths?

3. Make a list of ways you can work on improving your strengths.

4. Do you feel guilty about your weaknesses—those things you don't enjoy doing or don't have time to do? If they are not necessarily important, work on letting go of the guilt to allow you to feel more joy.

CHAPTER 6

Just an Average Story

Humble

"having or showing a modest estimate of one's own importance"

Wendy

THERE IS SOMETHING ABOUT LIFE that has a way of keeping you humble, particularly when you put yourself out there and open yourself up to criticism. It surely does for me. Do you have events that, no matter how much time has passed, you can relive the embarrassment of the day like it was yesterday? I certainly do. With each event, I can now say that I have grown in ways I never imagined possible.

How sad would it be if I had never experienced each of them? I often think that without them, I might not be who or what I am today. Each event has been responsible for my successes while keeping me humble.

I have always loved music. From the minute I was able, which was second grade in my school, my parents rented me a flute and a piccolo so I could play in the elementary school band. I practiced every single day. I was proud of my musical skills and my ability to play two instruments. I quickly became one of Mrs. Marshall's (my favorite band teacher) go-to band members for playing new music so others could hear how it should be performed.

By the third grade, I was chosen to perform a flute solo in the annual Christmas Concert. I was honored. My mom and dad agreed to attend the concert. This was a big deal for me and my parents. Although they never missed anything that my sister or I did as children, I knew that attending a concert was not something to which they looked forward. My mother had no clothes to wear, and while she never said it, I know she felt embarrassed by her appearance and her lack of clothing. My dad didn't really care what people thought of how he looked, but I know it wasn't easy for him to get my mom out the door.

They arrived at six pm to hear my performance. I peeked around the curtain to make sure they were there and to see where they were sitting. I could not have been more excited and nervous.

As I walked out on stage with my knees shaking, wondering why I ever agreed to this, I knew I was ready. I had practiced the song every day for months. Not only had I memorized this song, my parents had as well because they had to sit through endless hours of my practicing. I was halfway into the song when I missed a note and then couldn't find a way to recover. I knew it immediately and the audience knew it. I could tell by the looks on their faces.

As only a 7-year-old could do, I stopped performing and looked around with a look of sheer panic; trying to decide what I should do next. Should I run off the stage as someone had done earlier, or should I try the music again? Do I pick up where I left off or start over?

It was then that my mother's eyes met mine. She could tell, from the look on my face, that I was ready to cry (have I told you that I have always hated to cry?). As calmly as she could muster, she held up her finger in the number one gesture. She shook her head up and down indicating yes, all while pointing at me and holding up the number one.

I knew exactly what she meant. She was telling me not to give up and to try one more time.

I restarted the solo and performed it with perfection. This simple gesture by my mother gave me permission and the confidence to try again, despite a near failure.

What if she hadn't done that? Would I have ever taken a risk to perform again? Would I have auditioned for the New England State Band Competition and won a position? Would I have achieved First Chair in the band and performed solos throughout my high school career?

It is my belief that these types of experiences are presented to each of us to serve a purpose. They teach us that we can and do survive tough challenges in life. I understand in the scheme of life that dropping a note is not the end of the world. To a 7-year-perfectionistic girl, it sure did feel like it. These challenges are not what define us. Rather, the way we emerge on the other side speaks to our character and fortitude.

As I write this story 45 years later, I remember the fear, the sadness, and the feeling of failure I felt as a child. I also remember the feeling of accomplishment, success, and pride when I finished my performance.

You might think because I am telling you the story today that it continues to haunt my inner psyche. It would be so easy to perseverate on these negative self-messages—I failed, I made a mistake, I didn't perform it perfectly. After many years of self-talk and self-analysis, I believe events such as these are transformative. They reinforce my core belief that no one, including me, is perfect and that for as many successes as I have had, there have been as many failures. One doesn't happen without the other.

Retrospectively, I can honestly say that my most significant personal and professional growth happened as a result of my most significant failures. I also believe that moments such as these are imprinted in my brain to remind me that I human, I am not always going to be perfect (despite always trying), and that giving up is not an option. Perhaps the greatest reminders are those that also served to keep me humble.

In 1995, I was nominated, by a former college professor of mine, to serve on the board of directors of a nonprofit national continuing education company. I loved my role as a board member. It was here that I learned about planning and implementing continuing education conferences for nurse practitioners.

It was also during this time that I learned to speak professionally. My first engagement was early 1995 where I delivered a lecture to a national audience of nurse practitioners on anemia and laboratory interpretation. There were more than 250 nurse practitioners in the room. I was 28 years old, had been a nurse practitioner for only three years, and had never spoken at a national conference. I felt like an imposter. I was filled with fear and a lot of self-doubt. *What do I know about this topic that others do not? Why am I presenting on this topic?*

I remember her face; the nurse practitioner in the back of the room. She had long dark hair. She was angry, and she was visibly frustrated with me and my presentation. I wasn't even fifteen minutes into the presentation when she stood up in the back of the room and began shouting hundreds of questions at me (okay maybe not that many but it felt like hundreds). I did my best to answer her questions, yet nothing I said made her happy or content. I spent my entire one-hour lecture trying to win her over and please her; I ignored the 249 others in the room.

I managed to survive but left the stage in tears. I told my colleagues that this was the last time I was ever going to do such a thing; to put myself out there and open myself up for criticism. Fortunately for me (although I didn't think so at the time) they had other ideas. One of my colleagues responded with, "Too late, we already have you on the schedule for the same lecture in Chicago in a few months."

What would have happened if they gave up on me and allowed me to stop after that horrible experience? I had already given up on myself. Maybe I would have never presented again. Today, my career has spanned twenty-four years with more than 150 lectures each year. Speaking professionally is as much of my career today as being a nurse practitioner.

What came of this experience? It propelled me to work harder at my presentation skills and to develop my talent. I hired a professional speaking coach who helped me to learn to handle similar situations.

I have also done some self-reflection. I think this experience mirrors much of our lives. We spend way too much time trying to win over our critics and spend way too little time trying to keep our supporters. Experiences such as these have kept me humble and have allowed me to laugh at myself. Laughing at one's self is important and often cathartic.

Let me tell you about the time, while speaking in New York, that I took two steps back on a stage to get a drink of water. The problem was that the stage ended one step before. I fell backwards off the stage and only by God's grace did I land on my feet; all while wearing 3-inch heels.

After climbing back up on stage, I looked around at the audience, and every one of them had their hands over their mouths in sheer horror.

While I was horrified, I decided the best technique was to laugh at myself to give them permission to laugh. I proceeded to tell the room of 450 of my colleagues, "Phew, I have been dreading that my entire career, I am so glad that's over."

The roar of laughter is a sound I will never forget. To this day, people still see me and remark how funny it was and how well I handled it. I am humble.

Before you read on, I now must caution you. What I am about to say is quite graphic (for those not in the medical profession). You see, those of us in the medical profession can literally talk about any bodily function all while eating dinner.

Probably the most humbling moment in my career occurred in Cape Cod around 2015. The evening before, I had gone out to dinner and immediately began feeling awful. I knew I had contracted food poisoning at a local restaurant. In my world, we refer to this as a gastroenteritis. I was up all night with vomiting and diarrhea and of course, had nothing in the hotel to address these issues (one would never know I am a nurse practitioner).

I managed to pull myself together by seven am the next morning to head down to the conference center. Despite feeling quite ill, there is NO way to cancel a program such as this. More than 400 nurse practitioners had paid their hard-earned money to hear me speak for the next eight hours.

About one hour into the first presentation, I felt the overwhelming sense of abdominal cramping. I spent the next ten minutes arguing with myself about what I should do. *Should I tell the audience that I didn't feel well and needed to use the restroom, or just try to make it thirty more minutes until the break?*

I opted to try to make it to break. Unfortunately, the worst-case scenario happened. I had terrible diarrhea on the stage. It went all over the back of my light-colored tan dress. Thankfully, none went onto the floor.

One minute later (was it divine intervention?), the fire alarm sounded in the hotel. We were told to evacuate immediately. All I could think was, *I can't leave, I can't let anyone see me like this.*

Out of nowhere, one of the conference staffers appeared. I explained to her, in the most mortified voice I could muster, about my current situation. We developed a plan. She would back me out the side door; I would run to my room and change my clothes while the fire department was on their way to the hotel.

I didn't care about the hotel potentially being on fire— I had pooped my proverbial Spanx (I really did care, but I had more pressing issues and yes, I did have Spanx on).

This experience was incredibly mortifying so why have I told you this? Because, I also learned from it. I learned that I CAN SURVIVE! I can survive almost anything.

They say what doesn't kill you makes you stronger. I really believe that to my core. You can choose to spend life embarrassed by your failures or use them to enhance your skills.

I believe that this event has really given me an appreciation for patients who suffer from conditions such as irritable bowel syndrome and have had similar embarrassing episodes. I am truly a more compassionate and empathetic provider because of my experiences and because I choose to feel them, learn from them, and turn them into a positive life event.

So why have I opened myself up and shared with you these humiliating experiences? Mainly, because it is important to let you know that we are all human. Even those people who look so put together on the outside have made mistakes or have had embarrassing events.

While many people may choose to hide their experiences from others, I invite you to do just the opposite. Tell the world. Feel them. Learn from them. Stay human, stay real, and stay humble! These are qualities which are endearing and garner great respect from others.

Christine

For all the years I have known Wendy I have seen one consistent line of her incredible hard work, her self-awareness and her commitment to excellence. That was the same when she was young.

> *Wendy may forget until she sees the submission of this writing to our editor, but she was my middle school cheerleading coach, her sister and many of our friends were coached by her. It was then I learned quickly her incredible drive and hard work. She wanted us to perform perfectly and would make us rehearse over and over again. I recall her critiquing us and that it felt like she maybe wasn't happy with us, but then the most incredible thing happened. We performed one night at this opposing school and the entire auditorium went to their feet in a standing ovation and she was beaming. She congratulated us and she stood with pride and laughed and smiled at our performance. She then told us we should compete in the regional cheerleading competition and she told us she thought we were good enough to win. She told us it would take practice and commitment but would be completely rewarding. She convinced us all that we were worthy and so we entered that competition and we won. Her lessons, her pushing and her motivation lead us to a victory.*

I tell you that story because Wendy writes a series of stories that have stuck out in her mind and humbled her. Each one an embarrassing situation and each time a pivotal moment where someone or something helped her from completely crumbling and then a return to overcome the situation. In her story about her solo where she has to start over at her mother's assistance, I can actually see her mother in my mind. Her young mother who knew exactly what to do. Wendy may have been humbled, but she also showed up prepared, committed and willing to take risk. She also learned from her mistakes.

In this very writing, her willingness to share an embarrassing story is her level of human humbleness that she now carries with her from overcoming some tremendous things. These are the highlights because one thing I know, is to get where Wendy has reached, there is no question in my mind she has had to continuously overcome.

So while you will face moments in life where you are humbled, I want you to look past those moments and I want you to know that you will overcome and hopefully like Wendy in her stories, you will learn from them and you will also look out into the crowd and see someone looking back at you holding up the "#1" with their finger. Because we can always start over. We can always try again. Because we always have the strength to try one more time.

As for me, I am not sure I knew that as I dug out of my tough start in life and overcame it that eventually I would get caught up in the feeling of winning and filling my cup. I was so proud of my work at some point I didn't know I was bragging on myself, never realizing to the eye of a stranger I came off as the least humble person on earth. I thought the world could see how far I had come and yet, as if somehow my path was visible to the world when it wasn't. It took time and a lot of hurt for me to realize people didn't see me in that light. They say loss makes you humble and that is true. While I always feel I remained a nice person with the proper intentions, I would wave my flag of victory hard and high and I know that didn't help me with many people.

It's funny how this works. You are told to climb, to compete and then when you do and you win, you need to accept your accolades gracefully they say.

Well, let me tell you, that is not me. The person I relate to is the **Rudy** of the world. The ones who ran out on to the field with people crying and cheering from the stands. I am a fan of the underdogs. I love the ESPN back stories every Sunday before football. I love the Olympic back stories when those years come. I just love the story of the human spirit and triumph. We love that story and that story is my story. I am humble today because I have been reminded as an adult far long into my story of success that we can lose it all in a minute. I have watched my parents fall ill, nearly beyond their ability to survive. I have watched a sister fall ill and almost die. I have been humbled by many things in life, loss, love lost, financial loss, health loss, just loss that hurts and is hard to overcome.

Yes, being humble will come in waves of little reminders to slow your roll. To remind you that you are human and fragile, and life is not to be taken for granted. I am humble to the extent that given a podium today I am far more likely to share my stories of vulnerable over coming than of success. That is when you know that you realize that there are no finite victories. Just the one you won today. You must remain humble.

I have also been saved by many other humble men and women. I have learned from humble men and women who had more and said less. Men and women who didn't need the attention I required born out of a feeling of lack or bullying. I have learned that people are less excited than I am often about more extravagant things. So, I have learned that I am who I am. Dramatic, excitable, elated and bold. Humble doesn't really fit into that picture very easily, but now at this age, it does. It's a complete set of feelings like a 24-piece china set. I have collected it all and managed to protect it, put it in my china cabinet and can look back now and see how lucky I am to have a complete set.

I know though I still have lengths to go in this category. I know that for all the pains of embarrassment, for all the losses I've experienced there will be more. That notion is new to me, relatively speaking. So, with my future decades of life, I will go forth knowing that I can be brought to my knees when I least expect it. It won't slow me though. It won't make me so cautious I am not living or striving to live or thriving and pushing. No, I will go forth with humility but vigor. After all, from my *humble* beginnings I will always remain a person who knows real lack and real loss, something that many people will never know. Being humble will always be who I am inside even if folks don't think so.

I would tell people for the sake of teaching that remaining humble isn't something anyone truly needs to worry about because life and God has a way of ensuring that you do so, just when you break a stride and maybe have a full cup of confidence, something will happen to remind you that you're not all that. I have an entire encyclopedia of humbling events. I have learned in rising back up after falling that you will fall again. Interestingly that didn't make me not want to rise up again, or to the highest of heights I could reach, it just prepared me mentally for the next speed bump, pot hole or full on cliff dive and it probably slowed the bragging down too because I realized somewhere along that path that I would only stand to look foolish later on.

I think there is something incredibly talented about those successful people who can amass fame and fortune and not feel full, but rather pay it forward, share, teach, give and open up your abundance for others to enjoy and I feel that Wendy and I both represent people like that.

We have dedicated our lives to giving. Teaching and helping and as such I feel we have lived with an internal reminder of being humble, something no matter how long we are gone from Parade Road that we will both always have inside of us. The beautiful thing about it is that while others may look at where we once lived or grew in disdain that place still holds the most joyous of memories because they hold the memories of our youth, our playing years, our growing years, memories of our parents as young adults and time with our siblings and neighborhood friends. No one can ever take those memories and stain them with economical bias or segregation of any kind and tell us we had lesser of a childhood than the richest of children, because our rock forts and tree houses, our walking paths and dirt driveways were our kingdoms in the magic of our minds and we lived and thrived and grew there with the richest of love and devotion from people who are the most morally wealthy of people we know. Yes, we know what it really was like, but we also know the cycle of that poverty was broken by the hard work and instinct of four people who were not necessarily given an education on how to raise 5 kids but rather just an internal compass that would lead all the way to where we are today. Humility is at our core and it always will be!

About You

C. S. Lewis said, "Humility is not thinking less of yourself, but thinking of yourself less."

In today's world, many people view humility as a sign of weakness. In truth, humility is a heroic and underrated virtue, most likely because humility goes unnoticed.

The next time you meet someone who displays a quiet, self-confidence, look closer. This may be someone to know better.

Questions for Self-Discovery and Thought

1. Have you had life experiences that are embarrassing or humiliating? Have you told anyone, or have you hidden them from others? Try the following: tell a friend about them, and discuss the impact they have had on you, or try reflecting on the event and developing a plan to turn the event into something positive.

2. Do you know people who are something less than humble, who appear to be full of themselves? Do you believe it's an act, bravado to hide their insecurity, or are they truly overly prideful?

3. Are you humble? Think of an example of you being humble? Did you feel good about that feeling?

4. Do you feel the need to boast? Walk through life feeling assured of your own path and your achievements without the need for others' approval.

5. Do you put others before yourself and enjoy making others happy? Self-absorbed people tend to think about what benefits them, whereas humbled people enjoy contributing to the greater good, and believe that their purpose lies in contributing to others lives in a positive way.

CHAPTER 7

And That's Why You Should Pick Your Battles

Loyal

"devotion and faithfulness to a nation, cause, philosophy, country, group, or person"

Wendy

AS I SIT AND WRITE THIS CHAPTER, it takes every ounce of emotional strength I have, to put these words on paper. In my family there is (and always has been) an unwritten rule: Loyalty is essential; you don't talk about your problems nor do anything to disrespect your family publicly. While no one ever told me this, it is something that I grew up knowing.

When Christine and I started talking about this book, I made it clear to her that I would do nothing to disrespect my parents or embarrass them. When I told my mom that I had agreed to write this book, her first question to me was, "Will it be about me?"

To which I replied, "Yes it will."

Her questions didn't end there; I knew they wouldn't. I could see her mind working. Her next question was, "Will it say terrible things about me as your mother?"

"Mom, you were a great mother. You did the best you could with what you had, and I am grateful for all you have done for me. I will do my best to represent you in that light."

She thanked me and dropped the subject. She never asked me about it again. Unfortunately, my mom died during the year I was working on this book and wasn't able to read any of my chapters. But, as I agreed, I will do my best with this chapter to honor her memory, while at the same time, remaining true to myself and the reasons that we decided to write this book—to help others.

Mental illness is a chronic and terrible disease. Not only does it affect the person with the diagnosis, but it also has a significant impact on children, partners, and siblings. My mom suffered from depression for as long as I can remember.

As a child, I remember her getting angry or sad and then spending days in her room. I also remember not wanting to do anything to anger her because she would retreat to her room, and we would have to deal with the wrath of my dad. As a child, I didn't understand depression or what was happening with her nor did I understand why my dad seemed to cater to my mother.

As an adult, I now get it and understand why my dad did what he did. He was the one who had to deal with her depression day-to-day. My sister Becky and I would go to school, but he was with her every day. He was the only one who could get her to come out of her room when she was depressed and sleeping for days. He would offer to take her to dinner or out for a ride; anything to help her escape the sadness and **break the cycle**. Back then, I thought he was the only one who could help her. Later, when I became a nurse practitioner, I learned that in fact, she was the only one who could help herself. It took my dad leaving for her to realize that changes were essential and that she needed to seek help for her depression.

I was fifteen when I came home from school to find my Aunt Barbara alone at my house. This was unusual as my mom was always home when we got there. She told me that my mom was in the hospital from a suicide attempt. She was going to be okay but would need to stay there for a while to get the help she needed.

I could not believe that I had almost lost my mother. When we spoke about her suicide attempt, years later as adults, she recounted feeling so much emotional pain that day she tried to take her life that when she made the cut on her arm with a razor, she didn't feel one ounce of pain. I have never been able to understand the depth of that pain (thank goodness), but I have had many patients over the years who have told me the exact same thing. I have learned to respect how much pain she must have felt to want to end her life.

Approximately a month before my mom's suicide attempt, my dad had moved out. It was such a surprise to me; I didn't see it coming. How could he leave? I thought they had a great marriage; they never fought.

In hindsight, they never talked either. My mother was so devoted to making sure that my sister and I were taken care of, and she spent every weekend with my grandmother and her family, that she left my father to himself. He became involved in a national veteran's association; making new friends and connections that did not include my mother. She would tell me, years later, that she owned her part in their split; she needed to be a better partner and wife, and she wasn't.

I stood in our driveway and watched my dad pack up his things. It seemed like an eternity, but everything seemed to move in slow motion as I watched him load everything he owned into his van. I sobbed and begged him not to go. That fifteen-year-old adolescent became a hysterical, screaming young child.

I will never forget that look he gave me. I could tell from how icy cold his stare was that there was nothing left. He had made his decision. He told me to move out of his way and go back into the house. As quickly as that, he drove away. I had never experienced such sadness and the feeling of emptiness.

When my sister arrived home from school, I broke the news of mom's suicide attempt to her. She was just 12 years old. We were alone in our sorrow; my aunt had gone to the hospital to be with our mom.

We had no idea where our dad was or how to contact him. When he moved out, he did not give us any idea where he was going.

As soon as I finished telling Becky about Mom, she asked me how we would get to work each day or to school. I told her we would be fine; I would make sure of it.

That evening, we were scheduled to work at five pm. We were working at a local restaurant. I told her to get ready, and I would take us to work. I kind of knew how to drive (I was taking Drivers-Ed). We jumped into the car, and I drove us to work.

All evening, we worked. We didn't speak a word of what had happened. It was not something we spoke about to anyone. We were told when we were hired that when we came to work, it was a place to leave your personal issues at the back door; we were there to do a job, not discuss our personal issues. We understood, and were respectful of that rule, even as 12- and 15-year-old children.

Eventually, my mom was discharged from the hospital on antidepressant medications and with appointments for psychotherapy. She talked about her therapist years later and how he helped her to see that it was okay to get help and work on herself and her marriage. My dad joined her at some of her therapy sessions. Paroxetine worked so well for her that she would stay on that medication for the next thirty years.

We didn't really speak much about what transpired, but over the next month or two, our dad moved back home. They started to travel together and develop a partnership that would become a model marriage for the next twenty years. They made each other a priority and worked on finding a common love, not just for us kids and their grandkids, but for travel and friendships. Eventually, they decided to sell their mobile home and spent the next ten years traveling the United States in an RV. They talked about those days as some of the best of their lives. They held hands, danced, and kissed every day; things I had not seen them do previously.

While telling this story has been tough, it is important. It is important to recognize that those who are affected by a mental health disorder often don't recognize the signs and symptoms; my mom didn't. Those around them may see the illness but are often too scared to speak up; particularly as children. It is important to know that it is only by speaking up that people can get the help they need to make significant life changes. I have seen this, with my own family and also over the past twenty-five years as a family nurse practitioner.

I do believe things were different years ago; particularly with the stigma attached to mental health issues. When my mom and I spoke about her depression as adults, she would tell me that back in the 60s and 70s, this was not something you spoke about freely.

I am glad that we can speak about it more freely now; that teens can come into my clinic and tell me that they are sad or are feeling depressed before they get to the point of suicide. It is better, I believe, now than it was 40 years ago. We are not there yet. As people and as a nation, we still have work to do.

I believe the bravest souls are the ones who raise that red flag and say I need help. Only then, can things improve and change.

Is it hard? Absolutely! However, you never know how good things can and will be if you don't take the opportunity to get help before it is too late. My mom and dad and our whole family are grateful for their second chance at life, the help of trained therapists, and the benefit of newer medications. They single-handedly, along with the work my mother did on herself, saved our family.

In 2002, my father was diagnosed with cancer of the gallbladder and bile duct. At that time, he and my mom were living in a 40-foot RV traveling the country. While the lifestyle was wonderful for them, he also knew that a diagnosis such as this required that he and my mom have a place where they could settle, close to family, while he got the medical care he needed. Before he returned to New Hampshire, I made it clear to him and my mom that I would set up a room for them in our house, and he and Mom could stay there as long as was necessary or needed. We had just built a new home; one that was certainly not designed for a man in a wheelchair, but we would make it work; if he was willing.

He and Mom moved into our living room. We had a hospital bed brought in and a pull-out sofa so that he and my mom could sleep in the same room.

Over the next few months, it became clear that he was not going to survive this cancer; he and I both knew it. About a week or two before he died, he asked to talk with me one night while my mom was sleeping. He asked me to promise him that I would take care of my mom; that I would provide a place for her to live and make sure that she would be okay. He knew that she would not survive if left alone, and I completely agreed.

For the next seventeen years, Mom lived with me, my husband, and our son. We took her on many of our trips and vacations to give her opportunities to see the world she had never seen. It was a win-win situation for us all. She helped with the house, our son, and my husband while I traveled. She had a place to live and thrive. We all enjoyed our time together. There was never a question about what we would do with her when my dad died.

In December 2018, a few days after Christmas, I took mom for an appointment to have a manicure and pedicure. She loved this little treat, and I tried to make it happen every few months. It was quite difficult because she was in hospice care for end-stage COPD. On the way home, she told me that her death was near and that it was going to happen soon. The way she said it, I knew I needed to stop talking and listen.

She talked for more than ten minutes and told me so many things that I wish I was able to record. She said, "If you hadn't taken me in after your dad died, I would have not made it. I know it. Thank you for all you did. I had so much fun traveling with you. You took me on so many cruises and trips to Hawaii. I would have never gotten there, and I am so thankful. You need to promise me that when I am dying, you and your sister will not do anything to keep me alive. I don't want to live this way any longer. I don't want any services. I have already paid for my cremation, and the funeral home has all my paperwork. I have a little money in the bank that I have been saving, and this is what I want you to do with it."

I agreed to respect all her wishes and told her that I would do as she requested. She knew that she was dying, and within four days, she died peacefully with my sister and me at her side, just as she had wished.

To me, loyalty is important. I try to be loyal to my family and to my friends. While there are great things about loyalty, loyalty should not preclude us from suggesting that a friend or family member get the help they need. While they may not be receptive at the time or may perceive our confrontation as being less than loyal, speaking up may be the difference between life or death or living and just existing.

My mom was one of the kindest women you would ever meet. She was loyal to her family and her friends. She would have given anyone her last dime or the shirt off her back if she thought it would help.

So.... In writing this chapter, I am loyal Mom. I am loyal to you and your example. I know you would be so happy if one person reading this book got the help he or she needed before it was too late.

Christine

"Wendy, I have circled back and read this a second time. I am on a plane to Key West for both work and pleasure, and I sit here crying. Knowing your mother and father makes every word you've written beyond real. I am there with you as a 15-year-old begging your father not to leave. I'm there with you as you sit by your dad's side during his final days. I can feel him. I can see both of them. I hear your mother's words during that final car ride. And I am fully aware of you, in the midst of it all.

You have always been the strong one. I want to tell you I am proud of you. Being on a plane always seems to compel me to write. Maybe this time it's your mom sending you a message through me from the heavens.

I know what she would tell you, Wendy—that your words are more than just words. You have saved many lives, including hers. You truly are a life saver in the world. You are here to be strong for your loved ones, and you are here to save lives.

Your mother's words haunt me: 'You saved my life,' she said to the woman she birthed. Your mother saved her own life by having you. You were her greatest accomplishment. I hope you truly know that."

~ Excerpt from an email between the authors.

LOSING WENDY'S MOTHER during the year we spent writing this book was heart-wrenching. I fully expect no one to make it through this chapter with entirely dry eyes. My contribution to the topic of loyalty was written months before Wendy, understandably, wrote her own. At the time I wrote this, I had I just spent a weekend with my folks, who have been married for 50 years this past year. That is a life sentence in marriage terms. It's the product of loyalty and is the easiest and most shining example of loyalty I can point to in my life.

I have this critical character trait in droves. I am loyal. I am so loyal, that I have stayed too long in the game of life with people, with companies, with things that had out lasted their value and ultimately their return loyalty to me. Still, this trait has rendered incredible upsides as well. I would argue it renders all people incredible upsides.

I believe loyalty is an embedded character trait. It's a quality that keeps a person adhered to a situation or another individual despite the pros and cons. It's what marriages are supposed to be built on. It's the foundation on which partnerships in the workplace are built. It's what makes people see you as good or bad, for having or lacking this quality.

So how do you get it? You can't buy it. You can't acquire it or contrive it. You can, however, exude it and be it, and in return, you will have it from most affiliations.

When I was a little girl, I found myself seeing things through to an end. Whether playing sports, joining a club, volunteering for a role in student council or a committee of sorts, I always saw it through. I always knew my service required a start and end. That I would endure the timeframe to the end despite any bumpy road I may find myself on.

That lesson was learned early and reinforced often. When I asked to join something, my parents always asked, "If you join, you know you are going to have to see it through to the end, right?" They made sure, in their innate ability to set a good example, that I understood joining means commitment, and commitment means remaining loyal.

I would often find, after agreeing to their terms, that somewhere in the journey I would question this decision, but I hardly ever recall going to my parents and asking to quit. I knew, having committed verbally my pledge of loyalty, that quitting was not an option.

This 'no quit' trait is one I have carried with me to my adult life. I knew at 18-years-old, when on my own for the first time, that I would live by a strong sense of loyalty, but I never knew how much this single trait would carry me to unfathomable heights in my career and in my life.

Loyalty is a tricky thing. Not all have—or choose to embrace—loyalty in their dealings with others. I have felt the sharp pain of disloyalty on many a front in my life; In relationships, in the workplace, and in life in general.

See, that's the thing about being loyal, you are subject to interacting with less loyal people.

You will go through life connecting with people who will surprisingly shock and harm your feelings with their inability to stay faithful to you, or to a cause you're tied to. Finding your loyals is important. *Make your closest connections with those who share your loyalty ethic and who choose to live that ethic as you do.*

It took many years and suffering the pain of disloyalty before I learned this lesson, despite my mother's attempt to teach me. I remember the event quite well. I decided to break up with one of my very first boyfriends. And my mother grounded me!

I thought she was crazy. I couldn't understand why I was being punished. I could not see how my breakup had to do with anything she needed to be concerned with.

Nothing I said or did dissuaded her. She grounded me for two months. She was unhappy about the hurt that I had put on the boy. She wanted me to think about it.

For sixty days, I sat at home missing social events, staying in my room, and watching the world pass by. I was, quite frankly, hating my mother right then. Eventually, the hard time passed, and I was released from my 60-day prison sentence.

This time, perhaps because I was a stubborn, rebellious teen who had dwelled in my anger instead of asking myself why I was being punished, I did not understand or learn the lesson. The only lesson I thought I learned was to not tell my mother what was up in my life. I thought and acted like a spoiled brat.

For years that bothered me. Inside, I knew I had missed the point. I told that story, with me as the victim, many times. It would be years and years later, when I first experienced heartache myself from someone who was careless with my feelings, that I would see the reverse, that I would understand the lesson. I finally felt the pain I had put upon my past boyfriend. I was not the victim in this story, I was thoughtless and acted poorly, and my mother was wise enough to know, even though I refused to listen at the time.

I think the harsh grounding contributed more than I realized to my understanding of loyalty, even before I understood the lesson. We can teach our children to be loyal. We can set an example. We can make them look at selfish acts or hurtful ones, like my mother did. The question is, are we willing to toe the line and carry on a set of moral beliefs for the next generation coming up?

As a mother, I have passed on the loyalty qualities I find so valuable. I have raised my son with the same rules about joining. He, being a child, has not always learned the lesson right away. We have sat a few times in parking lots, facing baseball fields, where we watched his team practice because he refused to get out of the car. I remained steadfast in the lesson. His commitment meant being part of a team that he could not let down. It was agonizing making him sit in the car until every player left the field at the end of practice; and completely necessary that he learned how his commitment mattered, how his loyalty mattered.

He would soon realize that he had to practice and play every game (unless of course he was truly sick, which happened on the rare occasion). He would soon choose to practice with the team rather than sit in the car. I heard him tell his coach once, "I am not happy to be here, I am only here because my mother made me."

His coach, admirable as most coaches are, told him, "I know how that feels, and yet here you are. I am proud of you. Let's make the most of it shall we?"

Soon enough, he was off and running and playing.

Recently, he surprised me. As he has grown into a budding teen, he has chosen to continue playing sports. He asked to practice at home! That, to me, is the sign I've been holding out for. That is evidence to me that he is developing the type of loyalty and work ethic I hope he will embrace. He is becoming more responsible.

He is far more logical than I was at his age. I can tell him $X = Y$ and he will listen, think about it, and then when an intersection hits, he will act as in the lesson he absorbed with great belief in what was told to him. He is smart. And I believe he gets the loyalty lesson—without a 60-day sentence.

About You

Strong people are loyal. The characteristic is something taught and learned and then exercised. People like our parents had a hand in what made our country great.

The lessons of loyalty our parents handed through generations are a shining example of core values. Was the lesson easier to learn because earlier generations lived during a time when credit was lent on a handshake? When neighbors truly helped one another survive? When communities worked together to help their neighborhoods grow and thrive?

Loyalty is one of the greatest characteristics found in iconic historical figures; people loyal to a cause; people loyal to an army or a community or even a war; so loyal that they would commit their life to its cause.

Nostalgia aside, we need the value of loyalty in our society more now than ever before. The world changes. People change. It is our core values like being loyal that keep us strong and must remain true.

Great leaders are loyal, and great leaders inspire loyalty. Be the example of loyalty you want most to follow, and you will be the finest of leaders.

Questions for Self-Discovery and Thought

1. Are you loyal?

2. Can you be more loyal?

3. Who do you need to go say thank you to for being loyal?

4. Who was the last person who, for no reason other than loyalty, showed you a commitment?

CHAPTER 8

And the Dream Morphs

Grateful

"feeling or showing an appreciation of kindness; thankful"

Wendy

IT'S THREE IN THE MORNING, *and I am getting ready to head out for another work trip across the country. This is my 156ᵗʰ (literally) flight of the year, and I am tired. I am exhausted by the early morning wake-up calls, the flight delays, the crowded planes, and the uncomfortable hotel beds. I need a vacation and some time away to clear my head and recharge. I have nothing planned. I want to sleep. I need to find a way to push through. I can't do one more thing. I am going to collapse from exhaustion.*

How often do you have thoughts like these? For many, including me, they occur frequently. Unfortunately, I find it easy to get consumed by negative thoughts and get sucked into cycles of negativity, particularly when I am tired. It is also easy to spend time and energy looking for things in life I don't have rather than appreciating all that I do. Do you feel this way also? I suspect that many of us do, and that I am not alone in my thoughts.

Three or four years ago, as my husband and I were driving down the highway to spend an evening in Boston, I had an epiphany. Let me preface this story by telling you that I love cars, particularly expensive ones. My mom and dad used to tell me that I have always had champagne taste on a beer budget. During our drive, I noticed that many of the cars passing us were Mercedes, BMW, Maserati, or Porsche brands. I wondered, how can so many people afford these cars?

As I contemplated this question, I began to count how many of these expensive cars I saw and compared that number with the number of other cars, such as Toyotas, Nissans, and Chevys. As I began counting, I realized that the number of people driving these luxury cars was quite small. This made me wonder, why did I notice them, and why they did they stand out to me?

The answer is simple—because I was looking for them! I was looking for the things I didn't have.

> *That was my epiphany. I realized that I could choose to spend the rest of my life looking for the things I do not have, or I could spend the rest of my days appreciating all that I have been blessed with. I needed to make a choice, and I was the only one who could make that transformation happen.*

Sounds like a simple change, right? Well, it isn't. Like anything in life, in order to make a change, we must first recognize that a change either needs to or is wanted to occur. This is true with everything from healthy eating, exercise, or self-care. While writing this chapter, a colleague asked me, how do you accomplish all that you do? How do you do what you do and keep up the pace? For me, the answer was easy. I can do what I do and can keep up the pace because I love what I do and am GRATEFUL for all the opportunities I have. I never imagined, given from where I came, that I would be where I am today. That realization alone makes me appreciate all that I have and all that I have been able to accomplish.

I also really appreciate that there are millions of people who are not nearly as lucky and blessed as I am. I see members of my family who struggle with poverty, addiction, and mental health issues. As a family nurse practitioner, I see the extreme challenges people face every day in my clinic; a mom who can't afford to pick up the medication for her sick child, the man who has worked the same job for 40 years and has hated every day of it. Yet, neither can **break out of the cycle** because they believe they have no other choice and no other option. I see young adults, who have their whole life ahead of them, being diagnosed with a life-threatening condition.

Don't get me wrong, I also notice the successful people who wear designer clothing and drive those expensive cars. They appear to be so happy. But are they happier than the person who struggles financially?

I have learned over the years that the answer to this question is, not always. I have learned that financial wealth doesn't dictate happiness. While it may make some things easier, it is not the maker of happiness. Look at the stories of people who win the lottery. Many end up divorced, destitute, and miserable.

I AM GRATEFUL!

I am grateful to have a stable marriage of thirty-two years, a healthy 21-year-old son, a roof over my head, food in the refrigerator, a job I love, a car to get me there, and the ability to eat when I want, and pay our bills without worry. Yes, I have worked hard for what I have but so has the woman who has worked in a factory making minimum wage for the past thirty years.

Maybe I am grateful for the small things in life because it hasn't always been this way. At ten-years-old, I began helping my mom and dad by writing checks to pay their monthly bills. By age fourteen, I was balancing their checking account. One month, while paying their bills, I realized that after all the bills were paid, my parents only had a few hundred dollars left for the remainder of the month. A week or so later, they gave me ten dollars to go out with my friends. I couldn't help but think, they only have $50.00 left for the next two weeks. Despite this, they never let on that they were worried or that I should be burdened by their finances.

When I was 12 years old, I asked my mom for Jordache jeans and Candies shoes. Despite the fact that my mom wore the same clothes year after year (because she couldn't afford anything new), she said yes. However, she and my dad also informed me I would need to pay half the cost of my clothing if this was the type of clothing I wanted.

I didn't hesitate. I immediately found a job picking up golf-balls at the local arcade. I needed to be there by six am every Saturday and Sunday. Rather than asking my parents to drive me, I rode my bike to the arcade. I made $1.00 per basket of balls. Each day, I would bring home about $10.00 to $20.00.

Upon realizing that I wasn't going to have enough money for the clothes, I applied for a job at a fast-food restaurant. Making $3.00 per hour serving soda and ice cream, I thought I was rich.

When I got accepted and decided to attend Simmons College in Boston, my mom and dad told me that they couldn't afford to pay for the $10,000 per year tuition. I would need to take out loans and work to pay half; I immediately responded with, "That's okay. I will do that."

Dad always told me, "Hard work won't kill you."

He was right. It didn't kill me. It taught me the value of a dollar, the importance of hard work and commitments, and made me appreciate everything I had (because I had teeth in the game). Sadly, I don't think that all kids are taught this valuable lesson.

When I was 13 years old, I was invited to attend a sleepover and birthday party at the home of a classmate. I could not believe she invited me; she was so popular. Why would she invite me? I spent hours thinking about what to get her for a gift, finally settling on one of my favorite gifts, a book.

Her dad was a physician, and they lived in a home located in the center of town. I had passed by it with my parents many times. It was a beautiful home. After arriving, she invited me in and showed me around her house. I could not believe my eyes. It was huge, but what was the most impressive aspect to me was her bedroom. Her bedroom was on another floor, the second floor. We had nothing like this in our home.

The next day when my parents came to pick me up, I got into the car and proceeded to tell my mom all about the night. I told her that I had such a great time; we played games, listened to music, and danced. I also said, "Mom, they have stairs going up to a second floor. They live in a real house."

Without missing a beat, my mom responded, "You don't need stairs or a second floor. The trailer we live in is beautiful and you have your own room."

It was at this moment that I realized 1) we were poor and, 2) I didn't know it.

Kudos to my parents! How hard it must have been for them to meet our needs, even when they were consumed with financial worry, without my sister or me ever realizing how poor we really were.

Living in a trailer park was all I knew. My grandparents, aunts, and uncles all lived in the same park with us. Many of my friends were in the same park, as well. Christine was just down the road in a different park.

Today, I cringe when I hear people say the phrase *trailer trash*. People throw this phrase around frequently. Or maybe, I am sensitive and pick up on it. I can't help but wonder, is this what people thought of me and my family back then? For years, I never told a soul that I grew up in a trailer park.

Today, I wear it like a badge of honor. Why? Because telling my story might inspire others to know that your past doesn't define you. It is a foundation, one which might make the journey a little easier or a lot tougher. Yet, with drive and perseverance and people who believe in you, that foundation might just be the reason that you are propelled into greatness. I believe it inspired my success.

I have often wondered what people see in me that makes them recommend me for a board position, a speaking engagement, or a state or national award. As a young child, teachers would frequently ask me if I was interested in doing an extra project or joining an organization such as Project Gateway, a group designed to enhance the education for academically gifted children.

Why did my professors in college nominate me to be the class representative or for various leadership positions? I spent years wondering why until a few years ago when I decided to just ask a few of them.

The answers were the same from everyone. They all said that I "always said yes, was eager to engage, finished anything I committed to, and was grateful and appreciative of all that I was given." To this day, I believe wholeheartedly that these are reasons I have been given such opportunities.

I believe that happiness is determined by one person and one person only. That person is YOU!

Only you can make the choice to choose happiness. You see, even in the darkest of our days, there is always something for which to be happy and grateful. As a woman, I can choose to pine for what others have, or I can choose to be happy and grateful for all I have been given. I believe that it is the choice we make and what or whom we choose to compare ourselves to that ultimately influences our happiness.

We all have days where it is easy to get sucked into a cycle of negativity. Negative thoughts can easily build on each other, like, *I don't have that style of clothing, I don't fit into that size, I don't have that big house, my kids are not going to MIT, or I don't drive that exotic car.* These thoughts can be common and pervasive.

When I find myself sinking into that cycle of negativity, here is what I have trained myself to do. Maybe this will be helpful for others.

When I am sitting on a crowded and delayed plane, I take a moment to reflect and look around. I gaze out the window of the plane and think, many people have never had the chance to get on a plane and see what I am seeing. When I am exhausted and have worked a 16-hour day, I think, *well at least I have a job, make good money, and have a bed to sleep in.*

Christine

WENDY AND I CHOSE GRATITUDE as the focus of this chapter because we both believe it represents a huge part of why we've been successful in life. Let me take you back to the 1970s when I first recognized the immense gratitude I feel for the awesomeness of life.

But it did not start with gratitude. There were times when I was not grateful. For this book to be real and resonate with people, we must share the things that are not awesome about ourselves and how we turned those moments into something great.

I believe I was always appreciative of the wonder of life. I know my gratitude existed early in life. However, I also was protected from the real heartaches of poverty because I had two extremely hard-working parents who made personal sacrifice to ensure we had everything we needed.

I feel regret for a few past instances where I didn't show gratitude, where, in hindsight, I clearly should have. I have apologized to my parents privately, and now, these acts and my apology can live on in this book as a public statement.

As a young child, I wanted things, like every child. I was incessant in asking for stuff at every turn when we were kids; when grocery shopping, when going to Zayres, or The Globe, or the Dime store. Needless to say, I did not get all the stuff I wanted.

As I got older, the stuff I wanted became more expensive. I kept on asking, even though I knew I was asking for the moon. This is not to say my parents didn't get me things. We always had amazing Christmas mornings. Always. I remember many of them vividly.

I wanted a 35M camera because I was taking a photography class. My parents saved and saved to put that present under the Christmas tree for me. Was I grateful?

No. They gave me an automatic, not a manual SLR camera, and I was a brat about it. Upset, I ran to my room and made a big deal out of it. They were so excited to get this camera for me, and I spoiled the gift. It was an abnormally expensive gift for them to give. How I reacted was extra rotten and selfish.

They ended up taking the camera back to the store, added money and got me the camera I wanted.

I regret how ungrateful I was, how badly I reacted to their hard work. It was selfish. I know now, and maybe knew then, just how hard it was for them to get that camera for me.

I understand today how lucky I was that my parents worked their butts off for us kids. Eventually, I learned that if I could earn money, I could get stuff for myself.

Even so, some things were out of reach. I secretly felt pain over things I couldn't do. I was vividly aware I couldn't ask to go on the foreign exchange trips. My French class was going to Paris; and I loved French, my ancestors' native language. I was good at it, too. But I knew I couldn't go, and so I didn't ask.

By then, I knew my parent's financial bandwidth. I didn't ask to join the ski club or the golf club or anything that would render me needing equipment for which there was no money.

I felt internal pain over it, I saw myself a victim. I recall when I was a budding teenager telling my parents, "I hate you!" and lashing out to ask, "Why was I born into a poor family?"

Rotten words. Selfish words. Words I apologized for in time; yet hurtful and mean words that cut deeply into undeserving parents.

I meant my apology, too. I sincerely am embarrassed that I was so focused on material things. Peer pressure and societal stature can create self-loathing when you don't measure up, even in young children who have no life-skills or tools to express their emotions.

I found my value in accomplishment. From early on in school, I won awards. I competed. I did extracurricular work that gave me recognition. In this way, I thought I was telling the world, *I am worthy. I am valuable.*

It's unlikely that everyone saw this value in me but finding recognition in these activities helped me overcome the feeling of financial shame.

I came to learn how foolish the pecking order of school can be. Our parents net worth is not what defines societal worth, but God knows, telling that to a teenager is difficult.

I came to understand and began to live by my value system as a young adult, and it's pretty much how I measure the world still today, thirty years later. Ethics. Kindness. Hard work. Loyalty. Trust. Commitment. These are the qualities that make people great.

Yes, that is who I would become and what I use as a barometer for others. Money has little purpose in my self-worth and how I see others. I see many people who chase the dollar. I dedicated a lot of my life doing the same, thinking THAT would bring me happiness. And at my richest, I realized having material objects brought me no greater joy.

As I write this, I am less than a year into a brand-new company build out. I have earned less this year than any year since I became an adult, and yet, I am unreservedly happy.

I am working with great people, and I know our efforts will bring us a return to prosperity and the income I need and want as a wealth legacy for my son. Aside from doing something I love and that I'm good at, my son's legacy is truly my one compelling reason to work as I do now. I have proven to myself I could do it. I have obtained all the material things I ever wanted. I reached the financial mountain top. I enjoyed the journey and the view.

Now my gratitude is tangible. I appreciate people and things for their hearts and minds. I truly fell in love with movies, books, and real-life stories of people who inspired me in some way. Experiencing these shared life-stories often brought me to tears and led one day to an epiphany, realizing that I, too, have an amazing story to share.

I began to use my story to teach; to give hope, to educate and motivate. Yes. I realized that my suffering, my mountains to climb, have given me the greatest abundance.

I have been giving back or paying it forward, whichever way you look at it. I found my path, as so many people do, stumbling down a road I had been marching on.

It took a real break in my life and for me to be humbled before I found my way onto the right road. I have someone to thank for this, someone who is not on the right path, someone who isn't authentic or giving; someone who gave me a front row seat to watch as this person manipulated people, misused power, and took selfishly as an adult.

That person would open my eyes. I had turned a blind eye to unsavory activities, and then, one day I realized I was no longer the fourth grade Superhero confronting a bully. I was, an adult in a professional workplace, the witness doing nothing; culpable by inaction.

My conscience called on me to do what was right. I was so dismayed over the handling of the entire situation that I threw myself on a sword I never thought I would. I *called uncle* on a job I loved because it suddenly had a price tag that depleted my moral fiber.

I learned much about myself and the value of gratitude during this time. I realized my job—my work—was my life. To leave that work was like ripping the core of who I was from my life. It was vital that I replace my primary job with something equally engaging. Undertaking my dream job, despite all the difficulties and challenges in a startup business and no matter how risky or monetarily depleting at its onset, it became my safety line to guide me out of a dark place; that and the outstretched hands of incredible friends.

Ironically, despite the gravity of this intersection, this new path in my life is far more valuable and aligned with my moral compass and is filled with gratitude for having overcome the pain.

Doing what is right is hard. Doing what is right means not caring for material things. All the great stories we've ever seen written end with someone who has been willing to risk it all to do what was right.

Today, I have real gratitude for my journey. It has not been an easy one since I am wired to do what's right. Don't get me wrong, I am not an unsung hero or do-gooder with no faults. I believe my God-given purpose is to shepherd people to safety.

I know that may sound crazy. I have harnessed this purpose into a coaching company and put all my business knowledge into making it legitimate. Now I live every day in gratitude for my work and evil showed me the way. I thank Evil for showing up.

I would tell you that life changes us. Our perspective and vision changes. Our priorities change.

40 years ago, I cried myself to sleep on the eve of getting a new trailer, something the entire family dreamed of having. The one we had lived in was old and starting to break down, and this new one was special ordered by my parents and was an amazing upgrade. We were so excited the night we got the key, knowing it was to be delivered the next day, that my parents put us all in the car and drove us to the site where it sat.

In the dark of that night, I got to see my brand-new bedroom, and I thought it was blue. I exclaimed how happy I was for a new blue bedroom, and my mother informed me it was actually green.

I was horrified, green? How could it be? Why would it be green?

"The living room is blue," my mother said. "We can't have two blue rooms."

I would have a green room. I lay that night, an ingrate, crying over wall color and missing the true lesson—to be grateful for the brand-new home that my parents worked tirelessly to get for us. I was a child with small wishes.

Today, I am a woman with small wishes again; thousands of days in between, and I return to the small wishes in life. This time, I know the lesson and I live it. I am grateful now.

I've been grateful for a long time. I am grateful for every person who has played a part in my journey, good or bad, because it directed me to exactly where I am right now. I have broken hearts, and I have had my heart broken. I have many regrets that I can't fix. Coming to accept that reality was the hardest thing I've ever done.

I am grateful today, for every smile, every hug, every conversation and for the time I will be giving to keep giving back.

I am grateful, beyond words, for my son. I thank him for making me see life in a different way. Thank you to his father Jason Beckwith, for giving me him and for the many years we rode along together. They were beautiful years. I love you both dearly.

Jagger- I love you with all my heart. I will always love you with all my heart. You are amazing and beautiful, and you have an incredible heart and soul.

I am grateful for my family. I love you all; beyond words. Deeply. My sisters. My parents. My extended family on both sides. All of you.

I am grateful for my friends, my true friends who showed up when I needed you in life, who didn't run away when things got tough, for understanding me, for seeing me for who I am. Thank you for that. I love you.

I am grateful for a few key people in my life who have truly stuck with me through some tough stuff. You know who you are. If you ever were at my side when I was failing, falling apart, or struggling and you stayed with me or said words that I so desperately needed, I am beyond grateful, as I know that I could not have survived my pain or situation without your words, love, and attention.

To Cory Parker, who is my life partner and has been for nearly twelve years, words will never explain my gratitude for you and your support. You have allowed me to soar. You allowed me to be my dysfunctional, highly overthinking, ADD self. I have laughed with you, I have seen far off places with you, and we have experienced many ups and downs together. You've seen my career from a front row seat and have fanned the flames of my work. I thank you. I love you. You are incredible.

I have gratitude now. For that, I am thankful.

Live with gratitude and don't assume people know. Tell them. It is the greatest gift you can give. Even now, as I read the words I've written, I am not sure that I have told enough people how grateful I am.

About You

Being happy and grateful is a mind-set. Being grateful was a choice each of us made years ago.

It takes 21-days to make something a habit. Our challenge to you is this:

> *For the next 21 days, reframe the negativity. Stop the negative thoughts.* **Break that cycle** *of negativity, and you will be amazed at the changes you will see, not only in yourself but in those around you.*

Happiness and gratefulness are contagious. Make being happy and grateful the one contagious disease you want to spread!

Questions for Self-Discovery and Thought

1. Practice negative thought stopping each day.

2. Reframe the negativity and find something for which you are grateful.

3. Start every day by saying something for which you are grateful. Many executives start meetings by asking each person to say something positive, a practice that, over time, leads to more cohesive and happier work groups.

4. Happiness is contagious—make it the disease you want to spread.

CHAPTER 9

Dark and Disturbing Secrets

Dichotomy

"a division or contrast between two things that are entirely different, or are represented as being opposed"

Christine

I HAVE BEEN LIVING IN DICHOTOMY my entire life, come to find out; maybe not visibly to my own self but very much to the observing eye. I toggle between loving myself and hating myself. I am not sure that I even knew this until someone told me they could see it. Once I thought about it, there was little left to debate. I could see the dichotomy of my existence all the way back to my earliest memories.

This topic is going make me go deep, which of course is not a place I am a stranger too, but with the idea that going deep will drag you, the reader, down with me, here's me saying I apologize, and here we go.

Living is suffering. I've said it in many ways and many places. We are all suffering every day. Our ability to self-correct our course is truly the easiest way I can describe success. When you think about this, it will hit you square between the eyes like a rock. If you have feelings, are in touch with those feelings and of course give two nickels about how others feel, then you are suffering.

Right now, as I write this, I am worried about both my sisters. I've been super busy, and I haven't been able to check in daily as I would like to. One of my sisters is sick, has been fighting long-term illnesses. One of my other sisters is living alone, recently divorced, finding her way through life on an island. I feel for her. I want to make everything right for her. These are examples of the nagging thoughts I have every day.

I could sit here and write 100 thoughts that are concerning to me about things and people. And I am willing to bet that you have similar thoughts of your own. Perhaps it's what we do, how we choose to act (or not) that makes a difference.

What do I do with these thoughts? I organize them for starters. Prioritize them. One technique I think may be unique in me is that I talk myself out of the pain. I will tell myself it's okay; that whatever is bothering me is my mind's way of trying to sabotage my happiness. What ensues is a mental debate between natural thoughts of concern and nagging, negative thoughts. I think of this as my mind's auto pilot, a mental corrector of sorts.

I thank God for these internal questions I ask and the talks I give to myself.

I often wonder about how many others are like me in this way. I know that many are not, and I also know those who are. I try to surround myself with those who are like me in their ability to stay a course of positivity. And, I will add that the auto pilot mental corrector (APMC) has not been there for me my entire life, nor has it always showed up when needed. I have seen my APMC take the occasional break, or even vacation, and a few times took off for sabbatical I am quite sure. I am laughing writing this.

I know that there is no way for me to teach you, in a written chapter, how to make your mind correct itself from negative to positive specifically. What I can tell you is that we own the power of our mind. Learn to recognize your natural state of mind; BEFORE it digresses to a negative place. Make this the starting place for being self-aware.

You can imagine how much it takes to live as an inspirational person, or in my case, to choose a career of coaching people and helping them keep course. I chose Coaching for my dream job. Basically, I signed up to help others with their business and life struggles. I asked myself (of course), *How would I ever muster the constant energy and happiness needed? Where would I find a surplus of it for me to give to others?*

Well, the secret is, giving it away creates an endless supply for me. That is a profound truth, I mean that genuinely. The more I can help others stay on track mentally, physically, financially, and in life in general, the greater happiness I feel.

The word *worry* has two meanings: 1) To feel uneasy or concerned and 2) To seize something with the teeth and bite or tear repeatedly. Which do you think is the meaning I embrace?

My worry wart gauge is like the NASA shuttle countdown clock; in that it's always running to show the next time the rockets are going to pop off. It never really stops. I know it's going to come again, that nasty worry, that depressing thought, that debilitating horror of a thought that stops me dead in my tracks. Yes. I know it will come. It's only a matter of time.

I think this life of perpetual dichotomy between positive and negative feelings and thoughts makes me normal.

If you have never sat and pondered life, the meaning of life, the purpose of life as an adult, I urge you to realize that we are all living a dichotomy of sorts. If we allow our feelings to take the reins of our life, imagine where we would be right now.

I would be somewhere in Europe backpacking with a block of serious sharp aged cheddar in tow, a small bottle of red wine, water, sunscreen and a bathing suit, my favorite blanket, a good read, and a picked flower over my ear. My skin would be brown from the sun and my legs coated with dried sea salt on them from swimming. I would have many companions who made me laugh at everything and nothing at all.

I would be sans schedule, no airplanes, no meetings, no phone calls or the like. I would work for food, wake late, drink 5 cups of rich delicious dark roast, freshly ground coffee with heavy cream and agave blue plant sweetener.

I would draw, sing, write and journal. I would window shop in catalogues. I would take a nap in the middle of the day. I would binge watch every show I could never see as an adult due to the life I chose. I would play the occasional guitar or piano, even though I have never mastered either one.

I would live in an unconditional life that gave way to my spoils in a belief that this lessor stringent life would set me free from this over-burdened one where I have set out to be a superwoman and save the world. And yet, every day I forge deeper into the life of a would-be superhuman because it calls me.

Do you see the conflict? Yeah. I know I am supposed to help people with their suffering; that I was put on this earth to speak in large groups or one-on-one and make others realize how gorgeous life can be on the peripheral of or despite our hecticness.

My life works. My career is an obligation that gives me great enjoyment and is a means to a lifestyle. A lifestyle that becomes less and less important to me as every second ticks on the old clock.

I see my age lines in the mirror. Grey hair beckons itself back to its natural state every few weeks from the color I so rigidly dye it to every time it begins to fade. I see time when I look myself in the eye in the mirror. I see life lived, hurt, mistakes, love; in short—a life.

I see my dichotomy now.

The fairy tale has long since faded. It's been replaced with a wisdom life gives when we live long enough and listen hard enough. Wisdom has its own beauty, as real and raw as is this earth we live on. The longer I am here, the more in love I am with life and this world. I am in awe of the beauty in a sunrise, a sunset, a moonrise, a snowfall, an inexorable crescendo of waves crashing ashore. There is much to see in the world.

I believe that the true dichotomy of every person's life is that they have the life they built, whether planned or not. I believe that you, like me, may find yourself down a road of your calling and not necessarily in the life you dream of. My lofty ideas that I have some sixth sense of another dimension when it comes to people, healing, believing, is real, but what that manifests into I don't truly know. I feel it calling me, but I also feel the call of travel and far off places. I can't even describe it. I just feel it and I will go. I will.

It will probably never end because I recognize now, in reflection, that my calling to live a full, fast-paced life started when I was a little girl who was chasing life as if any moment the door was about to be slammed in my face.

Today, I am still chasing life with the same vigor. I am a person who wakes every day excited about what is coming. The endless roads I have run and continue to run, whether rushed, chasing, urgent, or leisurely, I travel with an inner pull in the direction I am now living.

I live with a feeling that I should get off the ever-rotating merry-go-round. What keeps me living as I am today in my calling and dichotomy, is people's need for me, my love that they desire, my spirit that they connect to, and my calling—a beckoning from people who need my support. And so, it is that I wake and live in the present of my world instead of running away. I grab my mental staff and I stand watch on the hill for the wandering nomad who I can herd into the safety of my world.

I understand that I am a strong one; that my lengths of strength have been tested; that I have knelt at my bedside, on my floor, hands clasped together in prayer, begging for mercy from a breaking heart, or an inexplicable pain brought on by an occurrence, a person, feeling slighted, feeling lonely or just feeling hurt. I have risen every time stronger than before, and able to recognize the same plight in others; able to help them, to guide them.

For today, I am the strong one. Not every day or week or year. Just today. Now. When you need me, until I can't be strong any longer.

Wendy

SEEING CHRISTINE'S WORDS ON dichotomy resonates deeply with me. Her chapter and her thoughts read like a day in my mind. How could she have known?

So many *tabs* are open in my brain, and my mind is continually moving from one commitment and task to the next. I have overwhelming feelings of love and then disdain seconds later.

I want to help a person to succeed but then wonder why he/she doesn't seem to be helping themselves.

One minute I am happy to be working on a project, and the next minute I am cursing that I ever agreed to something that I had no business agreeing to.

I love what I do, yet I have dreams of packing it all up and heading to an island in the Caribbean, where I turn of the phone and the internet and just read books until I don't want to read any longer.

I dream of going off the grid, yet I am so frustrated when my phone won't connect to the internet.

I thrive on the chaos and meeting deadlines and then am frustrated by how many deadlines I have.

At eight am, I am Dr. Wendy Wright, Family Nurse Practitioner, and by five pm, I am donning my pajamas and having a glass of wine.

Me and the life I have created are truly dichotomies. This dichotomy is okay. If we are all to self-assess, aren't we all?

Christine speaks about her APMC. While I have never referred to my mind in the same way, I too, have learned some strategies that I have honed for the past fifty years.

When negative thoughts or feelings creep into my brain, I have learned to do a lot of self-talk. I will tell myself, *Go to bed; sleep on your thoughts.*

It has taken me a long time to recognize, but I have learned that not reacting and taking time to respond, serves me well. Many nights, I am ready to throw in the towel, to give up, and say, I am done. I am both mentally and physically drained.

It is amazing what eight hours of sleep and the sunrise can do to my outlook. They say the sun rises daily to gift each of us a new start; a day to try it again. Each day is a gift and the sunrise assures us that we have another chance. Taking a night to sleep and recharge always gives me a fresh perspective on whatever was troubling me the night before. Somehow, it really doesn't seem as overwhelming as it did the night before.

> *I remember so vividly one night when Dillon was about 6 months old. I was back to work full time as a Nurse Practitioner. My days were long and the evenings even longer to finish up my charts and labs. Dillon was continuing to wake every few hours throughout the night.*

> *Eric and I decided a week or two before, to 'Ferberize' him; a technique developed by Dr. Ferber from Children's Hospital in Boston, to help children sleep. We followed Dr. Ferber's book to a tee. I knew intellectually that it was going to take 3-4 nights of no sleep, but I wasn't prepared for how mentally and physically exhausting it was going to be. To watch your son scream and not be able to pick him up was draining. I wasn't sure I would make it through those nights, but I knew that what we were doing was not working, and we needed to help him find a way to sleep.*

> *I was so proud of myself. I made it through the first night, but on night two, I thought,* This is it. I cannot continue to do this.

I went into his room and said to my husband, "I know why people get angry and shake their children."

It was such a scary feeling; I loved this child. I had spent 18 weeks in bed to have him. How could a smart woman and a loving mother have such awful thoughts?

My husband looked at me and said, 'Go to the basement and sleep. I will take over and get him to sleep.'

I felt so guilty about leaving him to my husband, but I just couldn't hear him cry one more minute. Within three nights, Dillon became the best sleeper ever. He could fall asleep in the middle of a party when we put him down in his crib. Today, as a teen, he continues to be the best sleeper (maybe better than I wish).

I felt guilty about my thoughts and feelings for years until I finally spoke them out loud to a friend who said, "The difference between you and someone who harms their child is you recognized your feelings, you asked for help, and you walked away."

Her eloquent words have saved me years of additional guilt and self-disdain. My lesson in life? That husband/self-imposed time-out saved me and us.

I now will walk away from my laptop at nine pm, even when I want to send off that email. I now know that the e-mail I send tomorrow will be very different than what I would have sent late at night.

If you will allow me, my recommendation. When something truly seems overwhelming, if possible, sleep on it. Take a night or two to sleep before responding. In today's environment, it is so easy to post on social media, shoot off an email, or send a text and then regret it the next day. Self-correcting, as Christine so beautifully describes, is imperative and essential in my life. I am truly not perfect although I really do try hard. I am a work in progress. I very much know what I should do, but like you, I am a dichotomy.

When I first began my career as a nurse practitioner, we had classes on maintaining that professional relationship with your clients/patients. We were taught that you need to treat your patients but maintain distance and be professional. You need to be objective and warm but keep your professional distance.

About two months after I opened my clinic, I was visited by an older patient who had been a patient in my previous practice. He had found me at the new clinic and made an appointment with me to establish care. I was so happy to see him, I hugged him and welcomed him to my clinic. I had taken care of him for twelve years, and I could tell that he seemed off during the visit. I stopped the visit script, put down my laptop and said to him, "I feel like something is bothering you. Can I help?"

He proceeded to tell me that he thought he was the reason I was no longer at my previous practice. I probed his reasons for feeling this way, and he told me that he knew he always liked to hug and kiss me when he arrived for his visit and thought maybe it had gotten me fired. He told me that he really enjoyed the hugs he got from me and the staff because it was the only human touch he ever got. He was genuinely distraught.

I told him that if hugging him and getting a kiss from him on the cheek would have gotten me fired, I would have done it a million more times and accepted the consequences.

His smile was so big, and tears began to fall.

Today, I am proud to say he has been my primary care patient for the past 27 years, and yes, he still hugs me every visit.

I am truly a dichotomy. To the outside, I may seem tough, but I have a heart. I hurt even when you don't know it. Being powerful or strong, doesn't mean you lack feelings. It doesn't mean you don't hurt or grieve. Strong women have a heart. And... it is okay.

How did this girl from the trailer park in New Hampshire not only survive but thrive? I am truly a dichotomy!

About You

Understanding dichotomy involves recognizing the power in the whole. While it may seem that we've been talking about opposites, this entire chapter is about what makes up the whole of each of us. The dichotomy we choose can be our strength or our downfall.

Do we choose to turn negative to positive?

Do we wallow in self-pity, or do we look for ways to take actions that change our circumstances?

Do we make a decision with all the information at hand, including the negative, or do we pretend all is good, or all is bad?

The truth is in the middle, in the whole.

Questions for Self-Discovery and Thought

1. Do you have an APMC, like Christine? Or do you subscribe to Wendy's practice of sleeping on it? Both are excellent tools. Consider what your process is when you make decisions or when you self-talk.

2. Today, when you feel like responding to the social media post or a co-worker's email, don't. Sleep on it. Try it. The results are often different. Another option is to write the email but don't send. Re-read it the next day. If it still resonates, then send.

3. Do you feel like you are a dichotomy? What in your life makes you feel that way?

CHAPTER 10

Who Says You Can't Go Home Again?

Brazen

"bold and without shame; endure an embarrassing or difficult situation by behaving with apparent confidence and lack of shame"

Wendy

I HAVE NEVER SEEN MYSELF AS BRAZEN, bold, or fearless. I am always full of self-doubt and ruminate on my weaknesses and fears. Apparently, and thank goodness, others are not able to see what is going on inside my head. It is only over the last few years and because colleagues have repeatedly said to me, *you are strong, you are such a risk taker*, that I have come to listen and believe. In hindsight, I now know that my life has always been about having to be brazen. I needed those traits to survive and persevere. Oh, don't get me wrong; I might have survived without them, but I suspect the trajectory of my life and my career would have been different. I just need to look around and see some of my childhood classmates and relatives; those who were less fortunate. They provide clues as to what my life could have been.

My sister and I didn't have much growing up by today's standard, but we always had everything we needed. We were not wealthy, but we were rich in so many ways. My parents always made sure of it. How did two young parents, neither of whom graduated high school, raise a brazen young woman?

My young parents were fearless and brazen themselves. They say kids learn from what they see and hear. I am no exception. I learned from the behaviors that my parents modeled. While they had options, they chose to have and raise me even through my mother was only 18 years old, and my father was a disabled veteran who was already wheelchair bound at the age of twenty-two. They pushed us to become educated even though they weren't. They encouraged me to leave our town and go away for college, even though they didn't. Isn't this what brazen is all about? They were brazen!

As my parents would say, if asked today, they didn't necessarily know what they were doing when they were raising me but, they saw something in me the day I was born. My mother repeatedly told me, throughout my child and adolescent years, how smart, motivated, and articulate I was from an early age.

My mom was convinced I could become whatever I wanted to become. She has repeatedly told me that nothing I have accomplished or done has surprised her. She always knew I would accomplish great things. My parents coached me, cheered me on, buckled up, and hung on for the ride. They let me soar. Is that not what parents, educators, or mentors are supposed to do? I think it is. We each come with our own genetic road map, but our environment and our mentors help guide our lives. I do believe that my parents played a big role in shaping who I have become. They allowed me to be brazen.

I recognize now that it does take a sense of courage to become a registered nurse at 20-years-old, to land your first position as only one of few bachelors-prepared registered nurses in a hospital and accept a job in the Intensive Care Unit working nights.

> *I vividly remember the third day on the job. I was approached by a registered nurse who had graduated from a three-year diploma nursing program. During our employee orientation, she candidly told me that as a nurse, her clinical skills, clearly, were better than mine. She stated that she had more clinical hours in school and that all nurses should be educated and trained the way she was.*
>
> *I was flabbergasted. How could someone say something like this to someone they didn't even know? How could one woman say this to another woman, both of whom were just trying to make it?*
>
> *After taking a few deep breaths and collecting my thoughts, I responded, "You are correct, your clinical skills are superior to mine. Your program really did prepare you very well, clinically. You should be proud of the skills you have. However, give me two years, and I will be your manager."*
>
> *And... I was.*

Brazen, yes!

I was solely responsible for critically ill patients on ventilators, being kept alive by the grace of God and current technology. These young, 25-year-old men were under my care because of motorcycle accidents and not wearing a helmet or because they were 80 years old and just had a cardiac arrest. At 21-years-old, I was telling families that I didn't believe that we were going to be able to save their mom but that together we would make her death as peaceful and loving as we could, despite how horrible the situation was. I still see families today of the patients I cared for thirty years ago, who remember my care and how I advocated for their loved ones. With each life experience, we grow and build our confidences. Each has enhanced my brazen nature.

It also took courage, two years later, to leave that job and head back to graduate school; leaving behind the only job I really knew. It takes courage to resign from a decent paying job without another job lined up, particularly when you are the breadwinner in the family. Some might call it reckless; I choose to call it brazen. So, if you have ever questioned whether you are brazen and capable of taking risks, just reflect on your life. I bet you have!

Life is full of risks and challenges. We all face them. What defines us is how we deal with them. I, like you, have had my fair share of challenges; days in my personal and professional life where I question, *can I do this one more day? Am I doing the right thing? Will I fail?*

For many of us, self-doubt is that loud voice that overpowers the voice of self-confidence. The voices of self-doubt and insecurity are often so loud they drown out the voices of self-acceptance. While self-doubt is important to ensure we have fully vetted a situation, it is often overwhelming, and for many, keeps us from doing what we should or could be doing.

After getting my post-masters certification as a Family Nurse Practitioner, I accepted a job in a family practice office working for a Family Physician. Together, we grew the practice. We were a team. My strengths were his weaknesses; my weaknesses were his strengths. I really envisioned that I would finish my career working with him.

For me, I created the perfect job in the perfect location. Two days a week, I saw patients in a rural community in New Hampshire while the remainder of the week I worked on my medical education business. As time marched on, the situation in the office became untenable. Over a two-year period, I began to wake up each Monday dreading the next two days. I provided feedback and worked with the management team. I tried using my voice, but no matter how much I spoke, the situation was not changing. While I loved my patients, the work environment was toxic. I needed to make a change. It was agonizing. The life I planned and envisioned was not going according to my plan. The place I saw myself retiring from was no longer an option.

We all face such decisions. Do I stay and find a way to accept the situation, or do I go because I can no longer allow my career goals to be compromised by others?

I resigned my position. I had no job secured. What was I going to do? My thoughts were, *How am I going to pay the bills. I had never done such a reckless thing. I compromised the financial future of my family. Why couldn't I just make it work? What was wrong with me that I couldn't just continue and make it work?* Those voices of self-doubt were so loud, they were eroding my confidence.

I am the oldest child, the first-born daughter. My life has always been planned. I remember at 4-years-old telling everyone I was going to be a nurse. I knew I would go to college and graduate school. I was going to work in an office and stay there for the rest of my career. Deviating from this plan was never in the cards. I have always honored my personal and workplace commitments. I am not a quitter. I am a fixer. If something isn't right, I can help. If people are not happy, I can make them happy. It was difficult to accept that this was clearly not true in this circumstance. So, I left.

Brazen, yes!

When the door closes, a window opens if you are willing to take that step. This career deviation opened the door for me to, along with my sister, open two-family practices. Today, we have 24 employees and 9 nurse practitioners. We now provide care to more than 6,000 primary care patients. We now create the work environment in which we want to work.

Are you brazen? Do you listen to negative self-talk? Are you full of self-doubt? Is it keeping you from your dreams?

Christine

THE DISCOVERY OF YOUR INNER VOICE often calls for brazen responses and actions. Wendy and I are both wired in a way that allows us to push aside our internal insecurities and act when needed. I've come to realize others perceive such action as bold. Having this ability, regardless of how it's seen by others, is a strength, not a weakness.

Like Wendy, many of my thoughts about dire intersections in my life and career seem more frightening in reflection. I, too, have realized the gravity of a situation in the rearview mirror.

Our inner voices tell us to move forward, to stop, to reverse direction even. It takes a strong person to hear the voice of doubt and still act, especially action that you know others may criticize.

I have always wanted to help people find their inner strength. People want to wave their flags high and hard at times, and I think it's a beautiful sight when they do.

There is much goodness in this word *brazen*. I admire and love people who have taken charge in life to overcome great obstacles. It's an amazing quality.

So many people do not hold themselves or others to any sort of standard, let alone come with the wiring to defend, to live in environments that would cripple the next guy, so if we must label this trait, *Brazen*, it seems fitting. Brazen stems from the words *brass* and *brave* and is an action word; boldness in action.

When I think back to my childhood wish book my answer to the question, *What do you want to be when you grow up?* was always, "A nurse!" That dream would never transpire for me. My path took me down a different road. Watching Wendy take her incredibly unlikely start into nursing to the heights of where she is now, a national treasure and advocate in her field, with literary and educational contributions of the highest level, is honestly something that movies are made of.

You couldn't write a come from behind story that started any further back or climbed any higher than this. She is brazen and thank the lord she is because imagine how many lives she has changed the course of because of her own quest for excellence. Not only in the lives she directly impacts in her family but those of her staff, her patients, and the countless hundreds who listen to her lecture throughout the country. One person, one brave person, making a difference.

Be Brave. Be Brazen. It can change a million lives.

About You

Brazen. Audacious. Risk. Bold. Daring. Do any of these adjectives describe you? Perhaps not entirely, but your answer should be a resounding YES! There are times in everyone's life when simply getting out of bed in the morning is a bold action. The defining and underlying characteristic of each of these words is action. Even the most shy and retiring person can follow a passion, of daring to dream, and risking all to make it happen.

Questions for Self-Discovery and Thought

1. Where would you like to be today? Are you doing and living what makes you happy? If not, what is keeping you from making this change?

2. Think of something that you have done that required you to be brazen. You are capable being brazen; why not do it again?

3. When the negative voices in your head start talking loudly and eroding your self-confidence, thought stopping is so helpful. Consciously, stop the thoughts, and replace them with positive affirmations. I am smart, I am strong, I can do this!

4. Are you overwhelmed by your current situation?

   - How do you eat an elephant? One bite at a time.
   - Make a list of tasks you want to accomplish today and start the process of checking them off. You will be amazed at the sense of accomplishment you feel when you have checked your boxes!

CHAPTER 11

We Took Flight on Parade Road

Persistence

"firm or obstinate continuance in a course of action in spite of difficulty or opposition"

Christine

DID YOU KNOW THAT THE SMOOTH LITTLE ROCKS that line the bottom of the creeks and rivers flowing all around the world were once jagged broken pieces of stone? They are softened by the flow of persistent water that continuously wears away at their edges; stone smoothed over by water, softened from its hardened original existence. It's hard to imagine how much water it takes to get a rock to be smooth like that; and it's arguable that it didn't just become smooth eventually one day in an instant. Rather, slowly, speck by speck, its hard existence was chipped away over time.

Persistence can make many things happen; unbelievable things, unfathomable things, incredible things, really. How does one know the victorious feeling of a hard-wrought win, or accomplishment unless they are willing to be the persistent tide that eventually reaches the shore and carves amazing things through small, ever evolving progress? The answer lies within the study of what drives you. It comes back to the core of who we are and what lies within the fuel banks we fill every day.

If your priorities aren't aligned with your why, that tank is never full. You will coast down the road headed in some direction, gain more money, and likely accolades along the way, but will you be present in your life? Will you SEE the world around you while you are doing it? And most of all, will you persist to that incredible level that lies beyond the finish line where the true miracles happen?

Philosophers will tell you successful people have stumbled upon the levers they pull to reach incredible heights. Perhaps out of an innately born drive or even out of a recovery from a traumatic incident or overcoming an obstacle or an emotional break that aligns their desire to succeed with true inner emotions while also testing and challenging them.

I was called stubborn when I was a child. I can recall my mother and father discussing with one another my relentless pursuits that they did not always approve.

I would join a club at school. They would see me pour myself into whatever it was, which on that end of the spectrum, was a positive attribute to my quest for education, self-betterment, inclusion, even discovery. I wanted to see my own boundaries. I am still testing them to this day.

Back then though, when I wanted something that involved my parents, I would ask and ask and ask with a level of pursuit that defied persistence; whether it was to go somewhere with my friends, to buy something, for them to take me somewhere, to join something or do something, if they said no, I would persist until I either wore them down or broke them.

Persistence is one of those things that people can see as a negative when they are on the receiving end. I didn't accept NO for an answer, early on. I recognized I had a power to persuade through persistence. I found it appealing to make a case, to articulate my reasoning and belief in something to win over the other person's mindset, and often I did and could.

And when I couldn't, I would walk away unsatisfied and in disbelief with an immediate intent to return. I never walked away feeling as though something was over, a door shut permanently or a dead end. To me, there were no dead ends. Sure, I would reach the end of a road sometimes, but I always knew I could turn around. I always knew not only that I had the ability to reverse directions, but that I had no time to squander if that road was not the right one. I must go find the right one, and off running I would go. Persistence takes resilience and an eye for the finish line.

As a child I could not even fathom where my life would go as an adult; how it would take shape. I just knew my best was called upon every day. I knew this as a small child. I took great pleasure and pride in my school grades. I worked hard on school projects, and if I was part of a school club or sports team, I gave it my all. I have a strong sense of mortality, meaning that I realize I am here temporarily. I know that in my one lifetime I can make a difference, substantially.

As a little girl, I can say that I didn't have lofty dreams of my adulthood, because I was too busy conquering that day. My rewards and life's spoils came in the form of things that you don't spend money to buy. I desired things, I guess, but I truly took pleasure in doing something great, in challenging myself to learn something new, in writing, in singing, dancing, laughing and making others laugh.

I realize now looking back, there were moments in my life where I understood my reality, that we were not a rich family. God works in funny ways, because here we were, amongst some of the richest wealthiest people in the state we lived in, and yet all that we saw with other kids was out of reach. They drove nice cars, they wore nice clothes, and they were headed to expensive colleges. Even the clubs at school were out of reach for us: the ski club, the foreign language trips, the golf club.

We watched from the sidelines, knowing full well our situation at home was not one where we could ask for money for such frivolous things. I saw the scarcity of my parents' closets. They lived with no waste, they sacrificed. Sometimes I realize, when looking back, that my life was simple compared to theirs. I was raised in a warm, loving environment by two people who had life far harder growing up than I.

We lived in true poverty, and I say this not to shame them, just the opposite. They truly are incredible, hearty and strong people. Teenage parents who still are together today. Again, through their persistence they forged a partnership to stand by one another and work as a team. The love they had for one another was deeper than any love they had felt or known elsewhere.

Sometimes, when I write about my shortages as a child, I feel it to be far less of a gravity than my parents own situation. Because of their work ethic, their persistence to get up and drive themselves from poverty each day, they were able to keep us safe, warm, fed, clothed, and gifted at all our holidays.

It is worth mentioning that my inability to have the greater spoils of my surroundings in the way of things outside of my reach, the pain I thought I felt or shame I guess, now that I think of it, was brought on by me not wanting to be viewed as less.

I would watch as other kids would celebrate with excitement the things they would join. I would read the words on the papers: *To be part of this club you must pay X*, and *X* was always way more than I would have ever asked my parents for.

Those are the only scars I carry from my childhood really, not the ones that maybe poverty brings on. I felt afraid as a teenager, to expose my family's financial situation. Schools should know how hard that is on children when they must turn in empty sign-up papers, sit out from events, groups, and clubs.

I know it shaped me. I know it created my ability to withstand and persist. I am noticing now as a parent, my own young teenage son having similar actions now and then, and I wonder if one day he will regret it like I do. I hope so.

Today, I persist and tackle the thing in front of me with a vengeance. Looking at my entire life, between my childhood and today, I see amazing accomplishments that could have only been achieved through persistence and resilience.

I have lost a few races, but very few, and when I did, I found another way to ultimately get where I was going. I have had some serious sidetracks occur on the road I was on, inadvertently, mainly by my own doing, that took work to correct, but I always corrected course. I never gave up, and I never left a job undone.

If I started something, I made a 100% commitment to seeing it through, and I expected the results to be superior. I have never wanted to be mediocre at anything. As I age though, I will admit, I am more comfortable now truly finding my reward in helping others be exceptional. I now live as a teacher to others who need that direction.

I am helping others find their persistence and to discover their winning ability to, slowly but surely, and without wavering, smooth the rocks in their own rivers of life. I will continue this pursuit to help other persist with, of course, great persistence.

Wendy

I OFTEN DESCRIBE MYSELF, when I am speaking on stage, as a *tick on a deer*. Okay, I suspect this is a reference that only someone from New Hampshire could understand. If you have ever tried to remove a tick from yourself or your animal, you know what I mean. I am nothing, if not persistent; frustratingly relentless. Don't tell me no. Don't tell me I can't do it! This makes me more driven. Well, unless it's something I don't like to do, like cooking 😊.

At 15-years-old, I began dating a boy who was three years older. We dated for almost two years. I was smitten by his charm. He was my first real boyfriend, and I was convinced I was in love.

Despite this, we shared a dark secret. He was both verbally and physically abusive. At that age, I thought it meant he loved me. At least that's what he said. When I would ask him why he did what he did to me or said the things he said, he told me that I made him angry. He did them because he loved me so much and didn't want to lose me.

I believed him with every ounce of my being. I was convinced I could fix him and us. I made excuses. He had a tough life, his parents were divorced, and his father had been abusive. If someone would just love him enough, he would change. I believed that if I just dressed the way he wanted and said the right things, the abuse would end.

I became scared to speak for fear of saying the wrong thing. I never knew what would set him off. I was scared to speak to other boys for fear that I would pay the consequences later. He slowly and subtly convinced me that my parents didn't really love me, and that they were just trying to break us up. He told me repeatedly that they just wanted to see our relationship end (which of course they did because they saw what he was doing).

My bedroom resembled a flower shop or a funeral home—dozens of flowers as apologies for every time he was abusive. I remember counting 11 dozen flower deliveries over a two-week span.

I became a person that I didn't recognize. That fearless young woman who was a straight-A student, on the honor roll, a class officer, and a high-school varsity cheerleader was gone. I no longer looked people in the eye, no longer smiled as much, and I moved out of my parents' home to live with my 19-year-old boyfriend and his parents.

As any parent would be, my parents were devastated. They tried to convince me to stay, but I knew it all. There was no reasoning with me. I was brainwashed. I thought they were terrible for all the rules they imposed. I was so smart yet so naïve and stupid. I fed right into his control.

He now had access to me 24 hours a day, 7 days per week. He began to dictate who I spoke to, how I dressed, how I did my make-up, and where I went. It became oppressive. I was suffocating.

I finally mustered up the courage to ask my parents to let me come back home. I told him that my parents were going to file charges if I didn't come back home. It was a total lie, but I knew that he was fearful of the police, and he would relent.

My parents agreed to my request but with the following stipulations: the same rules would be in place when I returned home, the same rules I ran away from.

I consented. It seemed like a fair price to pay for escaping the torture. For the next six months, I worked hard to regain my footing and my self-esteem. I worked to repair my relationship with my parents. I worked on advocating for myself, even when he would try to undermine me.

I finally got up the courage to tell him that I had applied to college, had been accepted, and would be leaving for Boston in the fall. It was the break I needed. He was furious, but I honestly didn't care. I was emotionally ready to save myself.

During the last month he and I were together, I became friends with Eric. We had been working at the same fast-food restaurant for the past four summers. We didn't really like each other much during the previous summers, but something was different that spring; the spring of my senior year in high school.

We talked after work and hung out with mutual friends. When he asked me out on a date, I said yes. On May 7, 1984, we had our first date. It was my parents' anniversary; that had to be a good sign.

As we drove off on our date, I looked back at my mom and dad. Their happiness was palpable. He was so handsome and came from a good family. He was in college, was polite, and respectful. He had a future. What a fun night we had. This was what a date was supposed to feel like. I didn't want the night to end. I came home that night and declared to my mom that Eric was the man I was going to marry.

We dated for the next four and one-half years and married in the fall of 1988. I will admit that at about the four-year mark, I told him it was time to make a decision. If he was not going to commit to marriage, then it was time for us both to move on. Thankfully, he decided to pop the marriage question. It only took a little prompting on my part. Today, we have been married for the past thirty-one years.

Have I told you I am a bit assertive? And persistent?

It takes persistence to escape an abusive relationship. It takes persistence to make a marriage work. Don't misunderstand me. Eric and I have had our fair share of arguments and even discussions about ending our marriage. There are days when throwing in the towel would be easier than working it out. It has been a lot of hard work; we come from different places. Yet, what has kept us together and fighting for this marriage, is our love for each other, our son, and the life we have built together. Persistence and devotion have gotten us here.

Persistence has been a trait of mine for as long as I can remember. As I was looking for a space to open my first family practice, I spoke with a number of physicians in the community about a potential location that I had found. They all told me the same thing, "You will never make it there. The hospital tried and failed. What makes you think you will be able to survive there?"

I don't know why, but it felt right. From the moment I walked into the building, a medical office that had been empty for more than four years, I knew it was the place. When it feels right, it's time to take that leap of faith. Since opening, we have grown from seven patients to more than 6,000 patients. It is the hardest job I have ever had.

It is tough to manage employees, handle a million-dollar annual payroll, deal with angry customers, and see patients in primary care for more than twenty-five years. If I am to be completely honest, there are days that I would love to walk away. It is just so hard. But a hard task or job has never stopped me before.

Persistence has gotten me here, and I am happy to be where I am today. I am perhaps the luckiest woman alive.

About You

Benjamin Franklin said, "Energy and persistence conquer all things."

Even the most ordinary people achieve extraordinary results when they persist in delivering quality results. Persistence is the root cause of success.

Here are eight traits of persistent people. Explore how many of these you claim and, perhaps more importantly, embrace those you have not yet mastered.

1. A discrete, measurable action plan
2. Capturing and using momentum
3. Taking immediate action
4. Giving and using team support
5. Using problem-solving processes
6. Regular evaluation and direction checks
7. Obstacles are overcome
8. Focus and drive

Questions for Self-Discovery and Thought

1. What is your plan for success?

2. Review the traits above. Do any of these describe you?

3. Which one or two are your strongest traits?

About the Authors

CHRISTINE BECKWITH

Christine *(Buffy)* Beckwith is an Award-Winning Executive Sales Leader who has spent thirty years in the Mortgage finance industry. Her life and career are the culmination of progressive success stories that reach all the way back to her childhood.

A Best Selling and Award-Winning Author, Christine branched out in 2018 to begin her dream job as the Founder and President of 20/20 Vision for Success Coaching and Consulting.

Having broken many glass ceilings in the Mortgage and Banking Industry, Christine now is a columnist for industry and professional magazines and is a special video correspondent anchoring the news and interviewing experts in her industry.

She is an advocate for women, dedicating a complete division in her own company to the cause of women, amongst other causes and communities she touches at a vast level.

Christine spends her days traveling the national speaking circuit, lecturing on topics including her expertise in finance, while sharing her personal stories of inspiration and motivation and delivering both tactical and practical advice.

Breaking mainstream in 2019, Christine has appeared on huge stages to speak, kicking off the year at the Miami Gardens Stadium with Gary Vaynerchuk Agent2021 as the *Real Estate Expert Panel Moderator*. She has spoken this year at the Anaheim Convention center in Los Angeles, The Hard Rock Casino in Atlantic City, NJ and numerous prestigious organizations and media companies.

Christine will tell you that writing, teaching, and speaking are at the core of who she is. She embraces her legacy work with a commitment to make a difference in the lives of professionals and youth everywhere.

Christine is a mother, a girlfriend, a daughter, a sister and an aunt, a home maker and a lover of laughter, good health, home and heritage. She calls herself a happy human.

DR. WENDY L. WRIGHT, FNP

Dr. Wendy L. (Hurd) Wright, FNP-BC, FAANP, FAAN, FNAP was born and raised in Meredith, New Hampshire by Howard and Carolee (Hoyt) Hurd. She was the older of two daughters and knew, from age four, that she was going to pursue a career in nursing. After graduating in 1984 from Inter-Lakes High School, Wendy attended Simmons College (now University) in Boston, Massachusetts where she completed a Bachelor of Science in Nursing, a Master of Science and a Post-Masters Certification as a Family Nurse Practitioner in 1995. In 2019, she completed her lifelong dream of graduating with her Doctor of Nursing Practice from the University of Alabama, Tuscaloosa.

Wendy's nursing career has spanned three decades. Today, she is a Family Nurse Practitioner and the owner of two, nurse practitioner owned and operated clinics within New Hampshire. Wendy and her clinics have won numerous awards, including: Top Family Practice Providers in Souhegan Valley, Top 20 Fastest Growing Family Business, and Top 20 Women-Owned Business in New Hampshire.

In addition to her clinical role, Wendy runs a very successful medical education company where she delivers hundreds of lectures to health care professionals around the world. She has been a medical media spokesperson for numerous companies and has appeared on radio, television, and in print magazines. Wendy loves balancing patient care with education. In 2018, she was voted by her peers as one of America's Top Nurse Practitioners. She was one of 10 NPs (out of 270,000) to receive this honor.

She is the recipient of numerous additional awards and was chosen by the American Association of Nurse Practitioners as the 1999 recipient of the New Hampshire State Excellence Award. In addition, she received the 2009 NH Nurse Practitioner of the Year and the 2014 Top 5 Women in New Hampshire Business Award. In 2005, she was inducted as a Fellow into the American Association of Nurse Practitioners; in October 2014, a Fellow in the American Academy of Nursing, and in March 2017, a Fellow into the National Academies of Practice.

Wendy has been married to her high-school boyfriend Eric for the past 31 years and has a son, Dillon—a college junior. In her free time, she serves as the Chair of the

Board of Directors for the Animal Rescue League of New Hampshire and is a mom to her rescue dog Sydney Louise, an Australian cattle dog.

This is Wendy's second book–her first is entitled Adult Physical Assessment Cue Cards which has been in print since 1997.

> *"It has been my dream to write a book that tells my story. This book was certainly much more difficult than my previous because it required me to dig deep into some thoughts and emotions that I had long buried. Today, my dream has become a reality.*
>
> *Christine and I are excited to share our stories with you. We hope you love them as much as we enjoyed writing them. While it wasn't easy to show a side of us that we have protected for so many years, we hope that our journey will serve as an inspiration for those of you who have or are dealing with similar challenges.*
>
> *~I believe we all have challenges; it is how we handle them that defines our success."*

A Blast from the Past

Memories of our Parade Road Days

Christine and Becky (Wendy's sister) as Cheerleaders
Wendy is the Coach (back row, middle)

Wendy's Exquisite Trailer Home

Christine, her oldest sister (Tammy), and a
friend in front of her family's trailer home

Christine after a school choral concert

Her mother's favorite picture of Christine

Easter Parade on Parade Road

Innocence, hope, and wonder at all the world has to offer

Christine & Wendy's sister Becky singing in a choral concert!

Wendy's mother Carolee getting her girls ready for school.

If you look closely, you will see a swing set in the background of this picture of young Wendy. Both authors have fond memories of swinging and their recollections spurred the discussion that led to the cover image of **Breaking the Cycle**. Both were delighted to find this image and share it here.

Made in the USA
Middletown, DE
04 November 2019